University of Vermont
Burlington, Vermont

Written by Kevyn Jonas Lenfest
Assisted by Alyssa Vine
Co-Authored and Edited by Kevan Gray

*Additional contributions by Omid Gohari, Adam Burns,
Christina Koshzow, Chris Mason, Joey Rahimi, Jon Skindzier,
Luke Skurman, Tim Williams, Bradley Wagner and Sara Ginsburg*

ISBN # 1-59658-187-5
ISSN # 1552-1478
© Copyright 2005 College Prowler
All Rights Reserved
Printed in the U.S.A.
www.collegeprowler.com

Special thanks to Babs Carryer, Andy Hannah, LaunchCyte, Tim O'Brien, Bob Sehlinger, Thomas Emerson, Andrew Skurman, Barbara Skurman, Bert Mann, Dave Lehman, Daniel Fayock, Chris Babyak, The Donald H. Jones Center for Entrepreneurship, Terry Slease, Jerry McGinnis, Bill Ecenberger, Idie McGinty, Kyle Russel, Jacque Zaremba, Larry Winderbaum, Paul Kelly, Roland Allen, Jon Reider, Team Evankovich, Julie Fenstermaker, Lauren Varacalli, Abu Noaman, Jason Putorti, Mark Exler, Daniel Steinmeyer, Jared Cohon, Gabriela Oates, and Tri Ad Litho, David Koegler, and Glen Meakem.

Bounce Back Team: Malachi McCaulley, Amanda Paquette, Andras Pokorny

College Prowler™
5001 Baum Blvd.
Suite 456
Pittsburgh, PA 15213

Phone: (412) 697-1390, 1(800) 290-2682
Fax: (412) 697-1396, 1(800) 772-4972
E-mail: info@collegeprowler.com
Website: www.collegeprowler.com

College Prowler™ is not sponsored by, affiliated with, or approved by the University of Vermont in any way.

College Prowler™ strives faithfully to record its sources. As the reader understands, opinions, impressions, and experiences are necessarily personal and unique. Accordingly, there are, and can be, no guarantees of future satisfaction extended to the reader.

© Copyright 2005 College Prowler. All rights reserved. No part of this work may be reproduced or transmitted in any form or by any means, including but not limited to, photocopy, recording, or any information storage and retrieval systems, without the express written permission of College Prowler™.

Welcome to College Prowler™

During the writing of College Prowler's guidebooks, we felt it was critical that our content was unbiased and unaffiliated with any college or university. We think it's important that our readers get honest information and a realistic impression of the student opinions on any campus — that's why if any aspect of a particular school is terrible, we (unlike a campus brochure) intend to publish it. While we do keep an eye out for the occasional extremist — the cheerleader or the cynic — we take pride in letting the students tell it like it is. We strive to create a book that's as representative as possible of each particular campus. Our books cover both the good and the bad, and whether the survey responses point to recurring trends or a variation in opinion, these sentiments are directly and proportionally expressed through our guides.

College Prowler guidebooks are in the hands of students throughout the entire process of their creation. Because you can't make student-written guides without the students, we have students at each campus who help write, randomly survey their peers, edit, layout, and perform accuracy checks on every book that we publish. From the very beginning, student writers gather the most up-to-date stats, facts, and inside information on their colleges. They fill each section with student quotes and summarize the findings in editorial reviews. In addition, each school receives a collection of letter grades (A through F) that reflect student opinion and help to represent contentment, prominence, or satisfaction for each of our 20 specific categories. Just as in grade school, the higher the mark the more content, more prominent, or more satisfied the students are with the particular category.

Once a book is written, additional students serve as editors and check for accuracy even more extensively. Our bounce-back team — a group of randomly selected students who have no involvement with the project — are asked to read over the material in order to help ensure that the book accurately expresses every aspect of the university and its students. This same process is applied to the 200-plus schools College Prowler currently covers. Each book is the result of endless student contributions, hundreds of pages of research and writing, and countless hours of hard work. All of this has led to the creation of a student information network that stretches across the nation to every school that we cover. It's no easy accomplishment, but it's the reason that our guides are such a great resource.

When reading our books and looking at our grades, keep in mind that every college is different and that the students who make up each school are not uniform — as a result, it is important to assess schools on a case-by-case basis. Because it's impossible to summarize an entire school with a single number or description, each book provides a dialogue, not a decision, that's made up of 20 different topics and hundreds of student quotes. In the end, we hope that this guide will serve as a valuable tool in your college selection process. Enjoy!

OMID GOHARI ◯ CHRISTINA KOSHZOW ◯ CHRIS MASON ◯ JOEY RAHIMI ◯ LUKE SKURMAN ◯
The College Prowler™ Team

UNIVERSITY OF VERMONT
Table of Contents

By the Numbers............................ **1**	Drug Scene............................... **80**
Academics **4**	Campus Strictness **84**
Local Atmosphere **10**	Parking.. **88**
Safety and Security **17**	Transportation **92**
Computers.................................. **21**	Weather **97**
Facilities...................................... **26**	Report Card Summary **101**
Campus Dining.......................... **30**	Overall Experience **102**
Off-Campus Dining **35**	The Inside Scoop....................**106**
Campus Housing **44**	Finding a Job or Internship **107**
Off-Campus Housing................ **49**	Alumni Information.................**109**
Diversity...................................... **53**	Student Organizations............**111**
Guys and Girls **58**	The Best & Worst....................**113**
Athletics...................................... **63**	Visiting Campus......................**115**
Nightlife...................................... **68**	Words to Know.......................**118**
Greek Life **75**	

Introduction from the Author

Throughout the years of my college career at the University of Vermont, I have not only seen my growth retrospectively, I have felt myself grow—in age and in experience. I had the most wonderful time as a freshman, sharing personal stories with new faces and barely-met acquaintances: it was a time for personal explorations amidst a plethora of curious "first years." Our pasts and our dreams poured out, often into the late night or early morning, while new thoughts and ideas flowed forth from our minds as we expressed our knowledge of books, classes, friendships.

Sophomore year was a difficult one for me—more so socially than academically. But talking with friends and professors assuaged my itch to transfer, and by spring semester, I was once again my normal self. I took classes that challenged me and made me immerse myself in books, but still made time for friends and occasional parties. Ultimately, it all culminated after final exams when I published an essay from one of my classes in a scholarly journal based out of India. I had discovered one of my newfound passions, post-colonial literature and theory, which has propelled me even further into critical and literary circles, and given me a glimpse into the world of academia.

And now, as I wrap up another year, even better than the last, I prepare for my senior year and prospects for graduate school—always aware of how far I have come from my beginnings. I truly believe that the University of Vermont has afforded me opportunities that I would not have received elsewhere. Despite my uncertainties in the beginning of my second year, I have no regrets about choosing UVM as my school; it has truly been a wonderful experience. And now, more than ever, I am undoubtedly a more open person, more accepting, more intelligent, and I have both my school and myself to thank for that.

Kevyn Jonas Lenfest, Author
University of Vermont

By the Numbers

General Information
University of Vermont
South Prospect Street
Burlington, Vermont 05405

Control:
Public

Academic Calendar:
Semester

Religious Affiliation:
None

Founded:
1791

Website:
www.uvm.edu

Main Phone:
(802) 656-3131

Admissions Phone:
(802) 656-3370

Student Body
Full-Time Undergraduates:
7,900

Part-Time Undergraduates:
1,466

Male Undergraduates:
3,973

Female Undergraduates:
5,261

Female : Male Ratio:
3 : 4

Admissions

Overall Acceptance Rate:
75%

Early Decision Acceptance Rate:
78%

Regular Acceptance Rate:
72%

Total Applicants:
10,456

Total Acceptances:
7,792

Freshman Enrollment:
1,923

Yield (% of admitted students who actually enroll):
24.7%

Applicants Placed On Waiting List:
931

Applicants Accepted From Waiting List:
364

Applicants Enrolled From Waiting List:
0

Transfer Applications Recieved:
1,082

Transfer Applications Accepted:
747

Transfer Students Enrolled:
439

Transfer Application Acceptance Rate:
69%

Early Decision Available?
Yes

Early Action Available?
Yes

Early Decision Deadline:
November 1

Early Action Deadline:
November 1

Early Decision Notification:
December 15

Early Action Notification:
December 15

Regular Decision Deadline:
January 1

Regular Decision Notification:
March 31

Common Application Accepted?
Yes

Supplemental Forms?
Yes

Admissions Phone:
(802) 656-3370

Admissions E-mail:
admissions@uvm.edu

Admissions Website:
www.uvm.edu/admissions

SAT I or ACT Required?
Either

First-Year Students Submitting SAT Scores:
97%

SAT I Range (25th – 75th Percentile):
1060–1250

SAT I Verbal Range (25th – 75th Percentile):
530–620

SAT I Math Range (25th – 75th Percentile):
530–630

Retention Rate:
82%

Top 10% of High School Class:
21%

Application Fee:
$45

Financial Information

Tuition (In State):
$10,226 per year

Tuition (Out of State)::
$23,866 per year

Room and Board:
$7,016 per year

Books and Supplies:
$832 per year

Average Need-Based Financial Aid Package:
$10,079

Average Self-Help Aid:
$6,138
(including loans, work-study, and other sources)

Students Who Applied For Financial Aid:
66%

Students Who Applied For Financial Aid and Received It:
56%

Financial Aid Forms Deadline:
February 10

Financial Aid Phone (According to Student's Last Name):
A-F: (802) 656-8530
G-M: (802) 656-8531
N-Z: (802) 656-8532

Financial Aid E-mail:
A-F: team.a-f@uvm.edu
G-M: team.g-m@uvm.edu
N-Z: team.n-z@uvm.edu

Financial Aid Website:
www.uvm.edu/financialaid

Academics

The Lowdown On...
Academics

Degrees Awarded:
Associate
Bachelor
Master
Doctorate

Most Popular Areas of Study:
Business   10%
Psychology   9%
English   8%
Political Science 7%
Fine Arts   4%

Undergraduate Schools:
Agriculture & Life Science
Arts & Science
Education-Social Service
Engineering-Mathematics
Nursing-Health Sciences
Business Administration

Full-Time Faculty:
974

Faculty with Terminal Degree:
88%

Student-to-Faculty Ratio:
14:1

Average Course Load:
15 credits (5 Classes)

AP Test Score Requirements
Possible credit for scores of 4 or higher.

4 Year Grauation Rate:
53%

5 Year Grauation Rate:
67%

6 Year Grauation Rate:
70%

Did You Know?

UVM stands for **Universitas Virdis Montis**.

Best Places to Study
Billing's Student Center, University Green (weather permitting, of course)

Sample Academic Clubs
Cycling Club, Outing Club, Student Government, Literary Magazine, Music Ensembles

Students Speak Out On...
Academics

> "You are not a number, and that is important. If you want help, it is there. If you want to be left alone, that is also an option. It is really about what you want."

Q "**I've heard good things** about the teachers from the English department and the Sociology department."

Q "Professors at UVM are interesting people, and in many cases approachable and receptive. My own experience has been limited to teachers with the school of Arts and Sciences, and primarily the humanities at that, but I've encountered a lot of professors with a **great commitment to teaching**. Few have expressed their own work and research as more important and urgent than our education, at least in front of the classroom."

Q "For the most part, I've found professors enjoy teaching, and are **interested and knowledgeable** in their field."

Q "The quality of the teaching **totally depends on your major.** I'm a chemistry major—I know it doesn't sound like much fun, but my teachers were awesome. I took Spanish too, but I really didn't care for my professor."

Q "Like any school, you will have both **bad teachers and good ones**. Most professors were easy to get in to see and to get extra help from."

Q "Let's just say that some are really, really good and some are just plain bad! If you find out that you have a bad teacher, you can often **switch to another section** within the first two weeks of the semester."

Q "My current major, art, is not considered a very reputable major to be receiving a degree from at UVM. But depending on what your major is, **UVM may be ideal for you**."

Q "The professors are incredible. I'm an environmental studies major with a political science minor, and my professors have had a **really positive impact** on my tenure at UVM."

Q "After my first year, I have had ten different professors so far, and I have been pleased with most of them, but only really impressed with two: Philip Baruth from my Postmodern Literature class—**the best class I have ever taken**—and Kevin Trainor from the Religion Department. Some classes have been borderline engaging, but only my English 85—Postmodern Literature—class was demanding intellectually, requiring a really unwavering work-ethic for success."

Q "I think that at UVM the quality of your teachers depends on the effort that you make to get to know them. If you want to see them and get to know them, **they are there to help**, but they won't put that much effort into getting to know you unless you make the first move."

Q "Professors are an **important part of learning** any given subject, but the subject itself needs to spark my interest, most importantly."

Q "I started out as a mechanical engineering major and liked some of my professors, but when I switched to physics, I found most of my **professors to be outstanding**. I have gone back to get my Masters of Education degree from UVM. The education department also has outstanding professors."

Q "Teachers here are **just like teachers at any other place**: you like some, you hate some. Some are helpful and friendly, others might make trying to get help feel like pulling teeth."

Q "For the most part I've had really good teachers with a few not-so-good ones, but **more good ones than bad ones**. The teachers are usually very helpful. I guess it also depends on what you're studying."

Q "The professors at UVM are excellent. Not only do they provide you with a quality education, they also serve as **mentors and friends** for the students. I have only had good experiences with my educators; they've been one-in-a-million."

The College Prowler Take On...
Academics

When a professor really enjoys an area of study, he or she will almost undoubtedly be an emphatic and effective teacher. Similarly, those eager to learn will be more successful when the material, and/or the teacher, excites and engages them. And indeed, this appears to be the case at UVM, where both professors and students approach their jobs with enthusiasm and dedication. Consequently, a huge percentage of students are happy with their professors. As a result, UVM students experience satisfying relationships with professors, enhancing their academic experience and the knowledge gained in the process.

The professors at the University of Vermont are primarily good-natured and sincere in their quest to share knowledge. Given that UVM is one of the lowest paying universities in the country, most students feel these professors are not in it for the money. So, while teaching style, or personal style, undoubtedly varies from individual to individual, the vast majority of UVM professors teach with a genuine passion. Like Vermont itself, especially Burlington, UVM teachers are often in a class of their own: a laid-back attitude takes precedence over high-strung, fast-paced living. Yet, while many professors share this casual mentality that comes with the territory of the Green Mountain State, none are without their roots. Professors here definitely possess personality, reflecting a variety of backgrounds resulting in many refreshing, unprecedented approaches to teaching. Some bring with them stories and life experiences from as far away as South Africa, China, Russia, or India, while others were reared right here in New England. Even though nearly all UVM professors are exceptionally qualified in their field, holding degrees from prestigious universities; most still take the time to learn your name, and on occasion, become your friend.

The College Prowler™ Grade on
Academics: B-

A high Academics grade generally indicates that professors are knowledgeable, accessible, and genuinely interested in their students' welfare. Other determining factors include class size, how well professors communicate, and whether or not classes are engaging.

Local Atmosphere

The Lowdown On...
Local Atmosphere

Region:
Northeast

City, State:
Burlington, Vermont

Setting:
City

Distance from Boston:
3 hours

Distance from NYC:
4.5 hours

Distance from Montreal:
2 hours

Points of Interest:
Lake Champlain
Church Street
Robert Hull Fleming Museum
Ben & Jerry's Factory
The Shelburne Museum
ECHO at the Leahy Center for Lake Champlain
The Flynn Theatre
Restaurants Galore
The Burlington Bike Path
The Long Trail

Closest Shopping Malls:

The University Mall is a couple miles down the road on Dorset Street in South Burlington. The Church Street Market Place also has a mall—Burlington Town Center—but the main attraction of this pedestrian downtown area is the numerous shops and galleries—ranging from locally owned Vermont enterprises to well-known franchises.

Closest Movie Theatres:

We have one movie theatre downtown: Merril's Roxy Cinema on 222 College Street in Burlington. Newly renovated, it now specializes in more independent films.

A little further away than Merril's Roxy Cinema in the opposite direction is Merrill Theatre on 1214 Williston Rd. in South Burlington, which provides easy access for the more mainstream movie-goer.

For those with cars, the Movieplex off of Shelburne Road—Hoyts Cinema 9—is a short drive away.

Also, The Outlets Cinema—a newly built theatre with digital sound and stadium seating—is at 21 Essex Way in Essex, VT

Major Sports Teams:

Alpine Ski Team (NCAA Division I), Nordic Ski Team (NCAA Division I)—both consistently rank among the top-five in the nation, often even first or second. For NCAA Division I sports we also have Soccer, Basketball, and Hockey, among others.

Did You Know?

Jon Kilik, after graduating from UVM in 1978, went on to produce several films including major hits such as **Malcolm X, Do the Right Thing, Dead Man Walking, and Pleasantville**.

5 Fun Facts about Burlington:
- Nestled in a valley on **Lake Champlain**, Burlington is between the Green Mountains of Vermont and the Adirondack Mountains of New York across the lake.
- Over 100 years ago, Burlington used to have the **busiest shipping port in North America**.
- Attracts national and international **artists, musicians, authors**, and others.
- **Largest city in Vermont** with around 40,000 full-time residents.
- Birth place of the world famous **Ben & Jerry's Ice Cream**.

Famous People from UVM:
John Dewey (1879)—renowned philosopher and educator

Libby Smith ('02)—professional golfer

Jody Williams ('72)—won the 1997 Nobel Peace Prize for her continuing efforts to ban landmines worldwide

Students Speak Out On...
Local Atmosphere

> "Vermont and UVM are really laid back; people are super chill. I absolutely love it here, and I don't want to be anywhere else."

Q "I knew from the moment that I stepped onto campus that it was where I wanted to be. I've had such an **amazing experience here**, and I'm bummed that I've only got one more year left—time flies when you're having a good time."

Q "The atmosphere is great. **It's Vermont**! Burlington has a few other universities in the area; their presence is mostly a positive thing. The commercial downtown area is beautiful, but the surrounding area—Vermont's natural setting—can be a nice place to visit, too. Check out Centennial Woods."

Q "Burlington is an awesome town; I really like it. Church Street is cool. There are other colleges around, so the **population is quite young**. It's a laid-back, hip sort of town."

Q "The atmosphere in Burlington is a laid back, **pretty outdoorsy feel**. There are other universities present. We are pretty close to the mountains and the lake; there is a ton to do. Stay away from the box stores in Williston."

Q "It's true that there are some cool people here, and that there are **beautiful green mountains** at your doorstep, but I feel kind of taunted by the mountains when I realize that I have a lot of schoolwork to do."

Q "The **atmosphere is excellent**. It is definitely populated mostly by college students during the academic year. Stuff to stay away from—nothing, really. Some of the stuff to visit includes Shelburne, Church Street, Lake Champlain, Smuggs, Stowe, Mount Mansfield, Camel's Hump, Magic Hat Brewery, the Intervale, New Alpha Baptist Church, Flynn Theater, Higher Ground, and the New England Culinary Institute."

Q "I would have to say that Burlington definitely has a cool environment, but I just wish there were more 'real' people that I could relate to here. Granted, I'm a music major—there honestly aren't that many people who are as dedicated to music as I am, but I still feel a slight bit of **alienation from this crowd**."

Q "Since Vermont is such a small state, and Burlington is the 'major city' you can sometimes find opportunities here that you couldn't find in larger cities—it's a great place to **get involved with the community**."

Q "If you are looking for things to do, Burlington is the place to be. Lake Champlain is awesome, and Stowe has the **best skiing in the East**."

Q "All I can say is: Burlington, city of the future!! I am not a Vermonter, New Englander, or from the east coast, and the atmosphere here in Burlington, and Vermont overall, is the reason I came to UVM. The tolerance, the crunchiness, the happiness, and the **unabashed liberal and free spirit** provide the necessary background for a college student: an atmosphere in which everything and anything is accepted and supported."

Q "The local atmosphere at UVM and in Burlington is unlike any other that I have ever experienced. There is so much to see and do here. Saint Michael's College, Champlain College, and Middlebury College are all nearby. Make sure that you **visit the Red Rocks** in the summer."

Q "Burlington is a **fantastic place** to go to college. The community's relationship with UVM is pretty good; distinguishing locals from those associated with the University is almost arbitrary. The downtown area is always bustling with students, street performers, and regular people too. Good shopping and good eating in a fun and beautiful setting, you can't go wrong. There are a couple of other colleges in the area, St. Michaels College and Champlain College. Meeting students from these schools around town is less common than meeting UVM students, given the comparatively dominant size of UVM's population."

Q "Burlington and the surrounding area have a lot to offer. Of course, the easy access to the ski mountains, as well as the Long Trail and other parts of the Green Mountain National Parks is a huge bonus. The Ben and Jerry's factory is nearby, so is the Vermont Teddy Bear Company, as well as several microbreweries; all offer fun and lively, interactive, and in some cases taste-testing, tours. A bike path runs along the lake for miles, connecting the waterfront to beaches and parks. These spots offer camping, barbequing, cliff jumping, and great views. Also, **Montreal is less than two hours away**. Everyone heads north for a night or two at some point."

Did You Know?

The **quality of life** in Burlington was recently ranked among the top ten cities in the country.

The College Prowler Take On...
Local Atmosphere

With majestic, rolling fields, golden stalks sweeping in the wind, and the Green Mountains hailing brilliantly in the background, Vermont is a visionary canvas for those who love rural landscape and the cycle of the seasons. Those who come to Burlington, though, will find a lively small city in the midst of the natural beauty. This is an obvious advantage for those who enjoy outdoor activities, such as skiing, hiking, or biking. For the outdoors person, Vermont boasts arguably the best region on the East coast for outdoor activities. While at UVM you can engage in numerous outdoors activities, and revel in the majesty of the Green Mountains. Nearby, the Winter months give rise to the East coast's best skiing at Killington and Stowe—the only Eastern rivals to Rocky Mountain skiing. The progressive community of both UVM and Burlington gives a revived or rekindled sense of place, proving that big things come in little states.

Burlington is a small but bustling city with about 40,000 people and five colleges, including UVM, in its vicinity. The birthplace of Phish, Burlington has an impressive music scene, gathering names from Ani DiFranco to Anoushka Shankar, and genres from underground hip-hop to jazzy blues. Some places that add to Burlington's flare are the Flynn Theatre, the place to be for a great glimpse into culture and performing arts, and the Fleming Museum, which offers a notable collection of artwork, most recently featuring Andy Warhol. The atmosphere of Burlington itself ranges as well, but leans toward "leisurely". People are mostly out to enjoy themselves, and strike a balance between work and play. On Church Street, Burlington's downtown pedestrian marketplace, a businessman bolting to the nearest financial institution is likely to see a dreadlocked guitar player performing for extra money. There's a little bit of everything in Burlington.

The College Prowler™ Grade on
Local Atmosphere:
A-

A high Local Atmosphere grade indicates that the area surrounding campus is safe and scenic. Other factors include nearby attractions, proximity to other schools, and the town's attitude toward students.

Safety & Security

The Lowdown On...
Safety & Security

No. of UVM Police:
33

UVM Police Phone:
(802) 656-3470

Safety Services:
Blue Light Phones
Safe Ride
RAD
Property Registration

Health Services:
Alcohol & Drug Services
656-0236

Athletic Medicine/Sports
Therapy 656-7750/656-7751

Counseling Center   656-3340

Health Promotion Services
656-0505

Help Overcome Problem
Eating (HOPE)   656-0603

Medical Clinic/Student Health
656-3350

Mindfulness Practice Center
656-3340

Nutrition Services   656-0603

Occupational Health Clinic
656-9788

Office of Conflict Resoultion
656-9788

Travel Health Clinic
656-3350

Woman's Health Clinic
656-0603

All numbers listed are area code 802

Students Speak Out On...
Safety & Security

> "Safety at UVM is great. Like any campus, UVM's campus has call boxes, campus police, and lighted walkways."

Q "We did have two girls that were assaulted, but it was late, and they were walking alone, which was a really stupid thing for them to do. Overall, I'd say it's pretty safe here, as long as you **use your head**."

Q "As far as I know, security and safety at UVM are top-notch. The campus police are actually a division of the state police, so **they're good policemen**, but if you do things like smoke weed in your room, they have a reputation for busting people, so watch out."

Q "**I've never felt unsafe on campus**; there are security personnel and emergency phone boxes around campus. It is not easy to get into most of the dorms if you don't live in them. Not all of the dorms are like that though. Mine wasn't, but I still felt safe."

Q "I personally feel profoundly secure and safe on campus, enough so to walk around alone anytime from midnight 'till 5 a.m. and not be worried. In case there ever is a problem though, there are **security call boxes** all over the place, so maybe there are some people that feel unsafe."

Q "For the most part, UVM's campus, as well as Burlington itself, feels safe and manageable. Incidents are generally well publicized and **security is dependable**, although perhaps campus police should be less discipline-oriented and more approachable with safety concerns."

Q "You don't hear much about bad things happening on campus. Safe Ride is a mode of transportation for people who need rides home late at night. UVM also has its own police force which **regularly patrols campus**. If you're a good kid, they'll leave you alone. If not, don't be surprised to find them knocking on your door."

Q "If you are male, you are safe. Females are fairly safe, all things considered. Compared to other cities and countries, this town and campus has to be **one of the safest ones**."

Q "UVM maintains a very safe campus. However, should a problem arise, we have 'blue lights' stationed all over campus. At the push of a button, a UVM officer will be at your service. UVM also has a fully trained police squad that is on duty 24/7. Our campus is very safe and secure. You'll always **feel comfortable here.**"

The College Prowler Take On...
Safety & Security

Many students love the secure feeling they get from having award-winning police services on campus. Many others, however, feel that the university police are an overbearing burden on their conscience. More often than not, these students' perception of police really just comes down to a fear of getting caught. Subsequently, those with nothing to hide are apt to have nothing to fear. While those sidestepping the law behind closed doors usually feel a bit more wary. Regardless of direct campus involvement, UVM naturally avoids many of the problems that exist at other colleges and universities that are set in cities. With little crime in the Burlington vicinity, there is little to fear from the outside community.

One possible reason for an increased comfort level may be due to President Mark Fogel, the new president of the university. President Fogel and his administration are responsible for an increase in the number of campus police. Although, be forewarned, the campus police are not simply "rent-a-cops". They hold the same jurisdiction and power as state police. In addition, there are "blue lights" dotting the landscape, serving as emergency phones should the need ever arise. Overall, however, UVM feels like a safe place, especially to anyone who comes from a city larger than Burlington—in other words, most cities. Some might feel that the police are omnipresent, especially those who get caught for alcohol or drug use, but that's the name of the game, and an aspect of colleges everywhere. There continues to be little crime in the area. So, as far as safety is concerned, it is a comfortable place.

The College Prowler™ Grade on
Safety & Security:
A-

A high grade in Safety & Security means that students generally feel safe, campus police are visible, blue-light phones and escort services are readily available, and safety precautions are not overly necessary.

Computers

The Lowdown On...
Computers

High-Speed Network?
Yes

Wireless Network?
Yes

Number of Labs:
7

Number of Computers:
685

Operating Systems:
PC, MAC, Linux and UNIX

Free Software:
Norton Anti-Virus, Adobe Acrobat Reader, Eudora, etc.

Discounted Software:
Available

24-Hour Labs:
Yes

Charge to Print?
Usually ten cents per page.

Students Speak Out On...
Computers

> "Most students do bring their own computers. Every dorm room is equipped with high speed internet. The network itself is generally pretty reliable."

Q "Since there are few labs located on the residential campuses, **having a computer is convenient and common**. Though labs do become crowded around finals, as a rule, if you have to wait at all, it won't be for too long."

Q "I definitely recommend having a computer and a printer because it is just a pain in the butt not to have them. I also definitely recommend using Ethernet because the school Ethernet connection **offers quick Internet access** and keeps your phone lines free, which your roommate will appreciate."

Q "**Definitely bring your own computer.** They provide you with an Ethernet connection to the Internet in your dorm. Ethernet connection is faster than a cable modem connection. It's just easier to do everything in your room rather than the lab."

Q "**The Internet is fast and furious**! Out-of-staters, bring your own laptop. I rarely use the computer labs, but when I do (usually the one in the Living/Learning Center on the third floor) it is not crowded."

Q "Computer availability gets **a little tight during finals**. I would bring your own computer. They have many great labs, but nothing compares to doing your homework in your own space."

Q "You basically can't survive without your own computer. Almost everyone at this school has either a desktop or a laptop, and there's probably an equal amount of the two among students. **The network is great**. We use a cable line which is so much faster than a phone line, and you don't get bumped off the Internet much. There hasn't been much complaining about the network."

Q "The computer network is usually very fast and very good. There are a lot of computers on campus, but I think that you will find that you want your own computer in your room. When we aren't doing work and stuff, we play **games on our computers**, or talk to people online. It is also very helpful to have your own computer for late-night papers and research."

Q "I say that you should bring your own computer. **Don't buy one from UVM**; it's a complete rip-off and the computers aren't very good. I got mine through the school—it's a laptop and I hate it. I repeat, do not order a computer through the school."

Q "Well, depending on the time of year, like during midterms and finals, the computer **labs are pretty busy**. It also depends on which labs you use. Some labs are busier than others."

Q "It's a lot more convenient to bring your own computer because all the dorms have Ethernet connections, so you'll always be online. We also **register for classes online** starting at 6 a.m., so having your own computer would be helpful for registration."

Q "Of course, try to bring a personal computer if possible. There are Ethernet hookups in all the rooms and the connection is very fast. **The labs aren't too crowded**, although the library can get that way at certain times of the semester."

Q "The school's pretty well-equipped where computers are concerned, but **it helps to have your own** if you can get one. The computer labs get pretty crazy at the end of the semester, so it's nice to have your own computer and not have to deal with that. It also depends on your major, and how much you'll actually need to use one."

Q "Bring a computer if you have one. The library is always crowded, but Aiken and Morrill are not, you have to know where to go to find **empty computer labs.**"

Q "If you can, you should definitely bring your own computer. It's just a whole **lot more convenient**, especially on cold, snowy days when you don't want to hike over to the computer labs. It's usually pretty easy to find a computer somewhere on campus unless it's finals week."

Did You Know?

Ben Affleck attended his first semester of school at the University of Vermont back in 1990.

The College Prowler Take On...
Computers

In a world of ever-increasing, rapid technological advancements, computers are becoming more and more essential. From daily business affairs to cash registrars, computers are everywhere, and UVM is no exception. It is not surprising then that nearly all students, as well as the university, recommend bringing your own computer. The university has an Ethernet connection which provides students with almost instantaneous results. They also provide at least one port per student living on campus—meaning everyone gets more than his or her fair share of Internet usage. Moreover, the Internet is "free" (for the low, low cost of your college tuition). But, at any rate, Internet use is unlimited and widely available around campus.

If you have your own computer, it is best to bring it. Without a doubt, you will be thankful in the long run. If you do not have one, or cannot bring yours for some reason, there are a number of computer labs available to students, and they tend to have sufficient capacity. Across the board, computers are usually in good shape. The Math and Engineering departments have much nicer computers and computer labs while the library settles for older, albeit still working, ones. Occasionally people complain that documents saved at the library pop up on their own computer only as gibberish. Always save your work to a disk, your email, the network, or any way possible! And as always, don't wait until the last minute, or you might find yourself in a waiting line that extends past your paper's deadline.

The College Prowler™ Grade on Computers: B+

A high grade in Computers designates that computer labs are available, the computer network is easily accessible, and the campus' computing technology is up-to-date.

Facilities

The Lowdown On...
Facilities

Student Center:
Billings STudent Center
ALANA Student Center

Athletic Center:
Patrick Gymnasium

Libraries:
Bailey-Howe Library

Theatre on Campus?:
Royal Tyler Theatre

Coffeehouse on Campus?
Cyber Café and Waterman Café

Bowling on Campus?
No

Bar on Campus?
Not yet (there has been inquiry into building one)

Popular Places to Chill:
Main Green
Redstone Field
Cook Commons

Campus size:
450 acres

Students Speak Out On...
Facilities

> "The Student Center is a great place to study; it has big, comfy couches. The athletic facilities are also great; they are accessible, free, and, depending on when you go, sometimes they are not crowded."

Q "The gym is pretty nice. I go almost every day. The **equipment is good.** There are lots of weights and machines to use, and it usually isn't overly crowded."

Q "All the facilities are great. **The gym is cool** because you can look out the window at the mountains while you bike or jog. The computers are all pretty new, and the student center is also nice."

Q "The athletic facilities are good as well as the computers. Billings is a pretty **awesome student center**."

Q "Most classrooms are nice, and the dining areas are clean. **People hang out all over the place.** The lobby of your complex will have ping-pong tables and pool tables and stuff, but most people hang out in their rooms or halls and just chill in there."

Q "The athletic center is really nice and has pretty much **anything you could want** from a climbing wall to a swimming pool. I don't know much about the computers, but the buildings are all really nice, and there is an ample amount of places for students to gather and do whatever they want to do."

Q "The athletic facility is nice and available to all students and faculty. I hear it is much **less crowded during off-peak hours**, especially mornings. There is talk of renovating the student center, which might make it a better study environment and place for campus activities. While there are a lot of important things going on in all areas of the building on a daily basis, students are less inclined to head there for study groups, or a snack, than other places on campus. I work as a night manager in the student center, and I can tell you that after about 9 p.m. the place basically clears out."

Q "UVM has great facilities. **The computers are great**. The Billings Student Center is really nice. It is in one of the older buildings on campus, but there are some plans in the works for renovations, and in the meantime, it's a nice place everyone passes through."

Q "The facilities are nice, especially the gym and weight room. The **student center is rather impersonal** and complex-like. It feels more like a maze than a place to go hang out. Computers, again, are available and usually not crowded, but most people have their own."

Q "The facilities on campus are pretty good. They are **up-to-date and working well**, and the administration is always in the process of updating things."

Q "The hockey rink fosters a real sense of competition and athleticism with its sweeping oval ceiling and bleacher seats. The **workout facility is really nice**, but way too small for an institution of nearly 10,000 students (undergraduate and graduate)."

Q "The Student Center is really great. I spend a lot of time there because I am a coordinator for a UVM volunteer program. The athletic facilities are average. I think that the **Patrick Gym could be bigger** because it gets really crowded sometimes when everybody is working out."

The College Prowler Take On...
Facilities

The University of Vermont is a fairly large school and with it comes a number of facilities available to all students, faculty, and staff. While some take solace in a morning run around the track, others may prefer to workout in the fitness center and enjoy the panoramic view of the sun burning away at the frost. Likewise, students may prefer to study among their peers in the library, or, immerse themselves in a book near the fireplace in Billings. Depending on your preferences, there is likely a little taste of everything for everybody; students concur that UVM provides them with a number of facility options ranging from the solitude of secret study places to the flurry of high-octane hockey games.

The athletic facilities at the University of Vermont are simply beautiful. This is due in part to the commitment of the school to provide its students with updated equipment. A few years ago, the university purchased dozens of new machines. Best of all, the whole facility overlooks the soccer field and offers unobstructed views of the Green Mountains. UVM also has a number of indoor basketball hoops, an indoor track, indoor tennis courts, and of course an ice rink. There is also a climbing wall and a dance studio; in addition, the athletic complex offers daily and/or weekly classes in cardio-jam, kickboxing, yoga, and others. UVM is in the planning stages of building a new student center that will compliment the already existing Billings Student Center, which currently houses numerous places to study, the university radio station, and club spaces, as well as the Vermont Cynic—the school's newspaper.

The College Prowler™ Grade on
Facilities: B+

A high Facilities grade indicates that the campus is aesthetically pleasing and well-maintained; facilities are state-of-the-art, and libraries are exceptional. Other determining factors include the quality of both athletic and student centers and an abundance of things to do on

Campus Dining

The Lowdown On...
Campus Dining

Freshman Meal Plan Requirement?
Yes

Meal Plan Average Cost:
$2,216

24-Hour On-Campus Eating?:
Not yet, but there are possible plans to build one within the next year.

Places to Grab a Bite with Your Meal Plan:
Harris-Millis
Simpson
Simpson Store
Cook Commons
Alices
The Marché

Student Favorites:
Marché, Cook Commons

Other Options:
The Underground, The Atrium

Students Speak Out On...
Campus Dining

> "Most of the food is fattening, but you will find lots of vegetarians here, so there's also lots of organic and healthy food. They have made improvements to the on-campus dining and there are some new places opening up."

Q "The food on campus is great. The system that UVM employs allows for a wide **variety of choices** for any kind of eater. We have two major dining halls in which you can use your dining points at the door, and then eat all you want from the typical offerings of pizza, French fries, hamburgers, garden burgers, a salad bar, bagels, breads and lunch meats, soup, pasta, grilled cheese, cereal, and a meal that changes for most of the day. In the morning, they offer waffles, bacon, sausage, potato tots or hash browns, omelets, and other breakfast foods."

Q "Besides the dining halls, UVM also has **food-court-type places** where your food is made to order. These places include the Round Room (which offers a wide variety of sandwiches made on your choice of bread), the Underground (which is similar to Subway), and Cook Commons—located on the main campus—which offers a rotating selection of Chinese food, fast food, a 'homemade' food place, and wraps, which are really popular and really good."

Q "Of the cafeterias on campus, I say that **Simpson is the best** because they offer Chinese food. If you're a vegetarian or vegan I would tell you to go to Simpson. There are also places on campus that are like pay-for-what-you-want things, like salads, pizza, or Chinese food, so there are a variety of places."

Q "If you are vegetarian like me, I have found that UVM is probably **more accommodating than most schools**."

Q "The food is atrocious in the dinning halls (except for the occasional clean salad bar). I ate in the Harris-Millis dinning hall maybe twenty-five times all year, and I lived in that very complex! **That's how bad it is**. Instead, I would amble on over to the Marché at the Living/Learning Center where the selection is a bit fresher and wider, but constant and never (EVER!) changing. Thank God for downtown Burlington. I will give credit, however, to UVM Dining Services for catering very well to the vegans and vegetarians all across campus."

Q "The food on campus is pretty good, but some places can be pricey. For regular cafeteria dining, I suggest Simpson Hall on Redstone Campus, and for grabbing meals on the way to class, or getting a quick meal in general, **go to the Marché** (which is a mini grocery store with a smoothie bar, pizza, and great salad)."

Q "I dig the food. The variety has really improved since I was a freshman—bringing a lot more a la carte options to different locations around campus. You gotta love all you can eat though. Harris Millis always has pasta, but the ambiance at Simpson dining hall is far superior. We have a lot of **vegetarians and vegans** here in Vermont, and they are acknowledged and provided for all over campus. Some recent developments have been huge hits, namely the Marché in the Living and Learning Complex, and the Library's Cyber Cafe."

Q "The food is decent, but not great. This year I used the carte blanche meal program which I honestly wouldn't recommend. This gives you unlimited blocks which allows you to eat at any cafeteria meal as many times as you desire. I found that an **all-points plan is more efficient**. It allows you to eat anywhere on campus and even allows you to order pizza."

Q "The food on campus is pretty good. A great place to eat is the Marché, which has everything from vegan entrees to pizza to gourmet, home-cooked meals, even groceries. It is most students' favorite place to eat. Also, the **Round Room and Cook Commons** are great places near the academic buildings to grab lunch or between-class snacks."

Q "The Marché is a hot spot, but only if you're a big spender. The quality varies from day to day with those items that change, like at the vegetarian counter, where sometimes a delicious tofu stir-fry is offered, and other times a sub-par grilled vegetable and olive wrap. There is also the daily fried food station serving chicken fingers, popcorn chicken, mozzarella sticks, that sort of thing. The dining halls are, well, dining halls. If that's your choice, **Simpson is decent**. I personally would take a wrap from the wrap station at Billings over almost any other UVM food offering. Round room sandwiches are good too, but expensive."

Q "Learn to **cook for yourself**. You will be better off."

The College Prowler Take On...
Campus Dining

The University of Vermont receives high marks from a lot of students as far as the quality and taste of food. Where it loses points, however, is either in its extent of overpriced food, its often unchanging menu at several of the dining facilities, or its noticeable lack of Kosher food (except during Passover). For some of the more independently minded or strong-willed individuals though (or those who simply love to cook), there are several cooking facilities in each dorm section. Unfortunately, this option is available primarily to upperclassmen (given that all freshmen are required to have a meal plan). Nonetheless, it is possible to do both cooking and dining-hall eating with certain meal plans.

The University of Vermont actually has fairly good dining hall food as compared with other schools. Taking the food for what it is—bulk-purchased, vitamin enriched, mass-produced cuisine—it is actually pretty tolerable, and, in some cases, pleasant. Everyone will have his or her fair share of complaints, but overall, they do a fair job. An alternative to the crowded Harris-Millis and the Simpson dining halls are a number of made-to-order areas including Alice's in the Living/Learning Center, Cook Commons & the Round Room in the Billings Student Center, and the Underground (near the pedestrian tunnel). These places offer wraps, sandwiches, and a variety of other tasty treats. Additionally, UVM has the Simpson Store on Redstone Campus and the University Marché in the L/L Center; these places serve everything from salads to entrees, and stock groceries as well. But don't expect any deals; a box of cereal often costs upwards of five dollars, and a pint of the famous Ben & Jerry's ice cream will cost a dollar more than anywhere else—over four dollars. And remember, the food is not meant to be the best food you've ever had; it is there so you won't starve to death. Though it probably does not beat your mom's home cooking, UVM does have a better-than-average food program.

The College Prowler™ Grade on
Campus Dining:
B+

Our grade on Campus Dining addresses the quality of both school-owned dining halls and independent on-campus restaurants as well as the price, availability, and variety of food.

Off-Campus Dining

The Lowdown On...
Off-Campus Dining

Restaurant Prowler:
Popular Places to Eat!

A Single Pebble

133 Bank Street, Burlington
(802) 865-5200

Food: Fine Chinese cuisine

Cool Features: This Chinese restaurant has won some local awards, and is considered the best Chinese restaurant in Vermont. Chef Steve Bogart's authentic recipes include Ants Climbing a Tree (a Szechuan dish of pork and cellophane noodles), dry-fried green beans, and mock eel (thinly sliced shiitake mushrooms). The only problem is getting a reservation. Hours: Daily 5 p.m. – 10 p.m

Al's French Fries

1251 Williston Rd., Burlington
(802) 862-9203

Food: Hamburgers, hot dogs, and fries

Cool Features: Wow, talk about inexpensive, college-priced food. Hamburgers are $1, doubles are $2, and a hot dog is $1.12. Of course there is an additional charge of twenty-five cents for bacon, lettuce, or tomato. There are also chicken wings and fingers, but these items are a tad bit more expensive ($3-$4).

Price: $2, this is not a typo

Big Daddy's
177 Church Street, Burlington
(802) 863-0000

They have great wings and they deliver.

Coyotes Tex-Mex Café
161 Church Street, Burlington
(802) 865-3632

Food: Tex-Mex

Cool Features: One cool feature is the Green Card. After ordering so many margaritas, you get points toward free food. Since 1992, Coyotes has provided great Tex-Mex food to the Burlington area. They boast all of their menu items are made fresh in our kitchens using Vermont products whenever possible.

Price: Around $10

www.coyotestexmex.com

Five Spice Café
175 Church Street, Burlington
(802) 864-4045

Food: Thai

Cool Features: Five Spices Café boasts great Asian foods from Vietnam, Thailand, Indonesia, Burma, China, and Nepal! They have beef, chicken, seafood, and even a vegetarian menu. Calling for reservations is recommended.

Price: Most main-course dishes range from $15-$20

www.fivespicecafe.com

The India House
207 Colchester Ave., Burlington
(802) 985-7800

Food: Fine Indian Cuisine

Cool Features: Right next to UVM, The India House offers takeout, delivery, and catering. It has been a fixture in the Burlington area for years. They are opened seven days a week, serving lunch and dinner. Call ahead for places to park, and check out the new website showing their menu online.

Kountry Kart Deli
155 Main St. Burlington
(802) 864-4408

Food: Sandwiches

Cool Features: Kountry Kart Deli offers the largest selection of fresh deli-made subs and sandwiches in Burlington. They sell homemade falafels, lasagne, overstuffed sandwiches, soups, milkshakes and much. Kountry Kart also offers is open 19.5 hours a day.

Hours: 7:30 a.m. – 3 a.m.

Kwans Chinese Food
65 A Patchen Rd, So. Burlington
(802) 862-0475

Food: Chinese

Cool Features: Kwan's features a dining room and take-out options. They also offer free delivery with any order over $10. Kwan's offers an inexpensive option for the Chinese food-loving heart in us all.

Price: $5-$8

Leonardo's
83 Pearl Street, Burlington
(802) 862-7700

Food: Pizza

Cool Features: Leonardo's delivers to UVM, and accepts meal points!

kwanschineserestaurantcom.
verizonsupersite.com

NECI Commons
25 Church Street, Burlington
(802) 862-NEIC (6324)

Food: Cosmopolitan American

Cool Features: NECI is the New England Culinary Institute, where chef-instructors and students from all over the world preparing food in state-of-the-art kitchens. Call for reservations.

Pacific Rim
Saint Paul Street, Burlington
(802) 651-3000

Food: Asian Cuisine

Cool Features: The low prices at Pacific Rim set it apart from other Asian restaurants in the area. There is spicy and mild food, that comes in a variety of dishes.

Parima
185 Pearly Street, Burlington
(802) 864-7917

Food: Thai

Cool Features: From pad Thai noodle dishes, hot or mild Thai curries, and those sauces based on coconut milk, lemongrass, and lime that were strangers to Vermont not so long ago.

Parima (continued...)
The decor isn't that of a typical Asian restaurant. Instead it has warmth from the natural woods and stained glass.

Hours: Open for lunch Monday-Friday 11:30 a.m. – 2:00 p.m.; Dinner Sunday-Thursday 5:00 p.m. – 9:30 p.m., Friday-Saturday 5:00 p.m. – 10:30 p.m.

Penny Cluse Café
169 Cherry Street, Burlington
(802) 651-8834

Food: Breakfast menu with a twist

Cool Features: Penny Cluse Café is a small restaurant which caters mostly to the breakfast crowd. The atmosphere is a clean, well-decorated farmhouse.

Price: $6

www.burlingtonfreepress.com/customers/pennycluse

Sneaker's Bistro and Café
36 Main Street, Winooski
(802) 862-9081

Food: American breakfast and lunch

Cool Features: Only serving Breakfast, lunch, and brunch, the diner-style food is relatively inexpensive, with breakfast hovering around $6, and lunches roughly a dollar more. A quick glance at the online menu and any breakfast lover will salivate.

Price: $5-$8

www.sneakersbistro.com

Stone Soup
211 College Street, Burlington
(802) 862 7616

Food: Healthy

Cool Features: Stone soup has an excellent salad bar and decent entrees.

Sweetwaters
118 Church Street, Burlington
(802) 864-9800

Food: Sweetwaters menu consists of: salads, fajitas, soups, burgers, and basically any type of meat that can be grilled.

Cool Features: Sweetwaters is housed in what was the original site of the Burlington Trust Company. Built in 1925, the building retains its original moldings, cornerstone, clock, and architectural appointments. What were once bank vaults have been converted into walk-in coolers in the lowest level of the restaurant. On the main floor of the restaurant, you can see the original iron bank security grates above the entrance to the atrium. They also offer a 100 percent satisfaction guarantee.

www.sweetwatersbistro.com

Tortilla Flat
317 Riverside Ave., Burlington
(802) 864-4874

Food: Mexican

Cool Features: Tortilla Flat offers many Mexican dishes that include: fajitas, chimichangas, quesadillas, burritos, tacos, and of course margaritas.

Price: $5-$15

Hours: 11:30 a.m.-10:30 p.m.

Closest Grocery Store
City Market/Onion River Co-op
82 South Winooski Ave.
Burlington
(802) 863-3659

Student Favorites

Late Night Food:
Kountry Kart

Best Pizza:
Leonardo's

Best Chinese:
Kwans Chinese Food

Best Breakfast:
Penny Cluse Cafe

Best Wings:
Big Daddy's

Best Healthy:
Stone Soup

Best Place to Take Your Parents:
A Single Pebble

Students Speak Out On...
Off-Campus Dining

> "Burlington is a great little city. No matter where you go on Church Street, you will be able to find a delicious meal within your desired price range. We are also home to Ben & Jerry's, the world's best ice cream!"

Q "My friends and I usually hit the **cheaper places like Halverson's** (a cute and good bar-and-grill-type place where your average meal is about seven dollars). But other than that, there are a number of other possibilities including seafood, Mexican, Italian, and Thai restaurants that are all good."

Q "**Off-campus food is awesome**. I like to go to Sweetwaters and the New England Culinary Institute. You can also order out; CatScratch is good for that though."

Q "It depends what you're in the mood for . . . Chinese? Indian? American grille? Mexican? Thai? Burlington serves up some **fantastic restaurants** to eat at; there is no need to worry when it comes to off-campus eating in this town."

Q "For the economic purchase, I usually either go Indian, at the **Shalimar or India House**—both of which are pretty good—or I'll pick up a Thai Chicken wrap from New World Tortilla, which has some of the best peanut sauce I've ever had the pleasure to eat. One of the best sandwiches in town is the red onion sandwich at the Red Onion."

Q "If you or your parents put money on your Catscratch account with your ID card, you can order from so many places! You can **even order from Dunkin Donuts** if you want! It's a really great thing."

Q "If you want Asian food, Parima and Pacific Rim are the places to go. Then there are **classic burger and pizza joints** like Mr. Mike's Pizza, Manhattan's Pizza, Rueben James, and Ri Ra's, to name a few."

Q "I could write a novel on eating out in Burlington. Burlington, and the surrounding area, hosts a **plethora of excellent restaurants**. Anything on or around Church Street is a sure bet. NECI, the restaurant affiliated with the New England Culinary Institute, is the perfect place to take the parents (or to be taken to by the parents, as the case may be). Halverson's is a personal favorite—cozy with a pretty basic menu. I recommend the California Burger. For the adventurous eaters who like a little ethnic variety, check out the Pacific Rim for very unique dishes at good prices, the Sunday brunch at the Indian Restaurant, and Parima's interior design is as amazing as the Thai cuisine. Oh, and all-you-can-eat pizza and wings at Manhattan Pizza is possibly the coolest thing in the world."

Q "There are great restaurants in Burlington. I like the Five Spice Cafe, The Vermont Pub and Brewery, The India House, and Wind Jammer are all nice places. **Big Daddy's is good** for late night munchies! It's open for delivery until 2 a.m."

Q "There aren't really any restaurants on campus, but downtown there is **Church Street, Burlington's claim to fame**. It has many shops and restaurants to eat at. There's great food down there!"

Q "The Red Onion, Sweetwaters, Ken's Pizza, **NECI—my absolute favorite**—Three Tomatoes and, of course, Ben and Jerry's, are some of my favorites. Of course, there are other places to eat, franchises like Outback and Applebee's. You have unlimited dining options in Burlington."

Q "There are some **really good off-campus restaurants**; just walk down Church Street until you find one!"

Q "City Market is the place to go for salad (and everything else, I guess). **City Market is Burlington culture at its finest**, and you'll love every second of it. The food is incredibly delicious and fresh, and it's a prime place for people-watching too. I have never had a bad meal in downtown, and, while it can be pricey, it is worth it. If you are with guests and want to impress them with elegance, go to "O", the new restaurant on the waterfront…great ambiance there. One cannot go wrong with sushi, Thai, or, of course: Ben and Jerry's!!!!"

Q "There are **lots of restaurants**; the best way is to experience them."

The College Prowler Take On...
Off-Campus Dining

More than anything else, students at UVM cannot get over the quality, the ambiance, and the choices of Burlington's plethora of restaurants and eateries. Nearly every cuisine from almost all corners of the globe are represented here, and it's one of the things that drives the college community into Burlington, and keeps them coming back for more. In a town with so many possible, and different, places to eat, it is hard for most students to pick an absolute favorite. And as far as choosing a place to eat, one student put it perhaps most appropriately, "The best way is to experience them". Even in this small town of Burlington, there is a big-city feel when it comes to the plethora of food establishments, and international dining.

As you begin you first semester here, off-campus dining may not seem like a priority. You'll have plenty of meals provided by the college, and it will appear to be abundant at first. However, your satisfaction with the school's food will begin to fade. And when this happens, luckily for you there are several very nice restaurants off campus ranging from eclectic ethnic dishes to traditional American fare. Each establishment has its own specialties. Whether it be a breakfast, night out with your new flame, or a night out with your parents, there are enough choices to keep the off-campus dining experience a pleasant one. Prices vary too, with dinners ranging from around the ten-dollar mark to well over twenty-five just for the main course. A couple of classics include Sweetwaters, Tortilla Flat, Parima, The India House, and Three Tomatoes. For sandwich shops, try The Red Onion and Stone Soup. The best advice: be adventurous and try new places even if you think you've found a favorite.

The College Prowler™ Grade on Off-Campus Dining: A-

A high off-campus dining grade implies that off-campus restaurants are affordable, accessible, and worth visiting. Other factors include the variety of cuisine and the availability of alternative options (vegetarian, vegan, Kosher, etc.).

Campus Housing

The Lowdown On...
Campus Housing

Room Types:
Single, Double, Triple

Students in Singles:
19%

Students in Double:
64%

Students in Triples/Suites:
8%

Students in Apartments:
5%

Dormitory Residences

Chittenden/Buckham/Willis Complex
Floors: 4
Number of Occupants: 394
Bathrooms: Shared by floor
Co-Ed: By alternate floor
Room Types: Singles and doubles
Special Features: Close to campus

→

Christie/Wright/Paterson Complex
Floors: 4
Number of Occupants: 416
Bathrooms: Shared by floor
Co-Ed: Co-ed by alternate room
Room Types: Singles, doubles, triples
Special Features: Most modern dorms/facilities on campus

Converse
Floors: Arranged in columns
Number of Occupants: 121
Bathrooms: Shared by floor
Co-Ed: Yes
Room Types: Singles
Special Features: Quiet, close to classes

Harris/Millis Complex
Floors: 4
Number of Occupants: 610
Bathrooms: Shared by clusters on floor
Co-Ed: Co-ed by alternate sides of floor
Room Types: Doubles, triples
Special Features: Dining Hall, close to Athletic Center, Spirit and Leadership Development Program

Jeanne Mance Hall
Floors: 5
Number of Occupants: 150
Bathrooms: Shared by floor
Co-Ed: Some floors co-ed, some floors single-sex
Room Types: Doubles
Special Features: Close to class

Living/Learning Center
Floors: Arranged in suites
Number of Occupants: 582
Bathrooms: 2 per suite
Co-Ed: some co-ed suites, some single-sex
Room Types: Singles, doubles
Special Features: Program suites

Marsh/Austin/Tupper Complex
Floors: 4
Number of Occupants: 412
Bathrooms: Shared by floor
Co-Ed: Single-sex floors
Room Types: Doubles
Special Features: Outdoor Experience

Mason/Simpson/Hamilton Complex
Floors: 5
Number of Occupants: 397
Bathrooms: Shared by floor
Co-Ed: Co-ed by alternate rooms
Room Types: Doubles, tripless
Special Features: Simpson Dining Hall, Simpson Store

Wing/Davis/Wilks Complex
Floors: 4
Number of Occupants: 470
Bathrooms: Shared by floor
Co-Ed: Co-ed by opposite sides of hall
Room Types: Doubles, triples
Special Features: Closest to shuttle stop

Students Speak Out On...
Campus Housing

"If you want a single, go to Converse. If you are more academic, try for Wright Hall. If you tend to be on the more hippie/crunchy side, go to Living/Learning—where you will be part of a community 24/7 all year long. If you want to party constantly, try everything else."

Q "The dorms with the smallest rooms are Chittenden, Buckham, and Wills; most people dread living there. You never can tell, though. I lived in Wills for what turned out to be my **greatest year of college**. I loved every minute of being in Wills. The 'nice' dorms are Christie, Wright and Patterson."

Q "**Living on campus**, I have heard good things about Redstone campus and bad things about central campus. Avoid Harris-Millis, live in Christie-Wright-Patterson."

Q "Living on campus is fun, but you'll **want out after two years**."

Q "Live in Harris/Millis your first year. I lived there my first year and I thought it was great. Athletic Campus is the place to be **during your freshman year**, and Redstone Campus is the place to be for your sophomore year. People who live on Redstone already know everyone else there, so it's easier to meet people when you live on Athletic Campus."

Q "The dorms aren't great. They are **all fairly modern**, but they're all fairly small as well."

Q "Living/Learning center is a dorm designed with suites that have their own balconies and two bathrooms for five or six people. The other dorms don't offer any variety as far as set-up—no suites or apartments. Other than the suites in L/L, the only options are your **basic dorm rooms**, so not my thing. I prefer to live off campus."

Q "UVM offers less dorm options than a lot of colleges. Freshman and sophomore year everyone is required to live on campus in dorm rooms, with extremely limited access to suites, and virtually no campus apartments exist. Other than a few small dorms on Main Campus, where classes meet, most students live either on East Campus, or Redstone Campus—ten and twenty minute walks to Main Campus, respectively. Rooms on East and Redstone are far bigger than Main Campus, plus those dorms provide the easiest **access to the dining halls**. Many people consider East Campus the place to be freshman year, but we 'Main Campus kids' know that there is no shame in living in the 'shoe boxes' of the Chittenden/Buckham/Wills Complex. The nicest dorms on campus are on Redstone, in the Christie/Wright/Patterson Complex."

Q "Dorms are dorms. I got stuck in a triple first semester on Redstone Campus, which is primarily the campus where the upperclassmen live, and I wasn't particularly happy over there. Second semester I moved over to Athletic Campus and lived in Harris/Millis. Those rooms are the biggest on campus. Definitely **don't live on Main Campus.**"

The College Prowler Take On...
Campus Housing

UVM housing options span a few different campuses. Main Campus, the Athletic Campus (also called East Campus), and Redstone Campus are the most popular. UVM's recent investment in the campus that used to be Trinity College, just across the road from UVM's Main Campus, has increased the availability of on-campus housing, especially for transfer students. Most people try to avoid Main Campus more than anywhere else because the rooms are small and cramped, but the students who get "stuck" there are not always disappointed. The smallest of the residential campuses—Main Campus—is almost exclusively freshmen, providing residents with a close-knit community for students as they begin their college career. Also, students on Main Campus have only a five-minute walk to class on those cold Vermont mornings! The Athletic Campus, consisting of two dorm complexes and the Living/Learning suite complex, is a little bit more of a walk, but the rooms are more comfortable and access to the Patrick Gym can't be beat. With suite-style set up, and two bathrooms shared by four to six residents of a suite, Living/Learning is a great option for many students. There is also a common area, which is similar to a living room and opens up to a small balcony. Why so nice? Well, those who opt to live in L/L must apply and be accepted to a program which subsequently entails extra work. The programs are usually fun though, so "work" tends to be worth it. A couple of popular programs include Pottery Suite, Holistic Health and Wellness, Photography, and Readings in the Humanities. Redstone Campus, with pretty nice rooms, study areas, and facilities, has traditionally been where sophomores choose to live, despite the fifteen-minute walk to classes. Most dorms at UVM, however, do have adequate places to study for those who get stuck with a roommate who never studies at all. Additionally, every room is hooked up with free cable and high-speed Internet connection.

UVM does not offer many alternatives to the basic dorm room, with the notable exception of Living/Learning. The required two years of on-campus housing allows students to develop important ties to UVM, both socially and individually.

The College Prowler™ Grade on
Campus Housing: B

A high Campus Housing grade indicates that dorms are clean, well-maintained, and spacious. Other determining factors include variety of dorms, proximity to classes, and social atmosphere.

Off-Campus Housing

The Lowdown On...
Off-Campus Housing

Undergrads in Off-Campus Housing:
48%

Best Time to Look for a Place:
Six months prior to desired move-in date or earlier

Average Rent for a Studio:
$500/month

Average Rent for a 1BR:
$700/month

Average Rent for a 2BR:
$1,200/month

Popular Areas:
Anywhere within proximity to campus

Students Speak Out On...
Off-Campus Housing

"After sophomore year, almost everyone moves off campus. You can walk to anything in Burlington. Houses are everywhere; it's really easy to find a house to live in, and many are beautiful, huge Victorian-style houses!"

Q "Off-campus housing is right down the hill, which is really convenient, and **there are shuttle buses** that go down there."

Q "Freshmen and sophomores live on campus, and most juniors and seniors live off campus. Since there are no real options other than your standard dorm room for on-campus housing, moving off campus is definitely worth it. Between Main Campus and downtown, the hill is densely populated with big, old **houses transformed into many apartments** overrun with students. Much of sophomore year is consumed with apartment-hunting for the following fall; it is stressful, but necessary."

Q "It depends on you, but I went to boarding school and so I have spent a lot of time in dorms, and **off-campus housing is way worth it** and not too hard to find."

Q "Off-campus housing can be placed into one of two categories. The first is the group of housing located near campus in Burlington that is both expensive and of poor quality. **Housing is in demand here**, even without college students, so it's tough. Further away, the price isn't as bad and the places are nicer, but then it gets tougher to get to campus—so it's a toss-up."

Q "You can't live off campus until you are a junior. But if you plan on living off campus, you need to start **looking for friends to live with** and a place to stay no later than February of your sophomore year. Housing availability in Burlington is less than one percent this year, so you can't afford to wait. However, you get first dibs on on-campus housing as a junior and senior, and if you become a RA your housing is free."

Q "I think you have to wait till the end of sophomore year to live off campus. I think it is worth it, although **living on campus is nice** for two years. It is convenient too; there are plenty of options available."

Q "I'm in the midst of trying to acquire off-campus housing. There is **quite a bit of it available**, but you should start looking for it early—unlike me."

Q "Housing in Burlington is fairly expensive, and sometimes it's hard to get a good location because all of the students want to live between UVM and downtown Burlington. My boyfriend lives there and has a pretty nice place. The city of Burlington is very pretty and any house you get will **almost always be a nice one.**"

The College Prowler Take On...
Off-Campus Housing

With few exceptions, UVM makes you wait until you are a junior to live off campus, but when the time comes to move into an apartment, students often find it to be a pleasant change of pace from dormitory life. If you begin looking early enough, off-campus housing is convenient, fun, and certainly well worth it, according to most students. While most students jump at the opportunity to live in an apartment with their friends somewhere off-campus, not all elect to do so. Some stay because they enjoy the proximity of living on campus, while others are wary of the stress it may take to move away—bills, groceries, landlords, etc. Burlington is pressed for housing, so look early and make arrangements with friends for living together.

With an apartment also comes a large responsibility that often includes a commitment to a year lease. Try to think of whom you could live with as opposed to who you want to live with. Yet for those willing, ready, and able to move off campus, the biggest problem encountered is availability. Available rooms in Burlington can be few and far between. One reason for the housing crunch is the city's desirable qualities; another is the population of students already living off campus. Juniors often stay in the same place for their senior year, and those who don't often get a jump on a nicer place through friends, or their current landlord. It is fun to live in an apartment, but living several miles away from school, or the city, can be an entirely different story.

The College Prowler™ Grade on
Off-Campus Housing: B

A high grade in Off-Campus Housing indicates that apartments are of high quality, close to campus, affordable, and easy to secure.

Diversity

The Lowdown On...
Diversity

White:
95%

Asian or Pacific Islander:
2%

Hispanic:
2%

African American:
1%

American Indian:
0%

International:
1%

Out of State:
61%

Political Activity

Political activity on campus has a noticeable presence. There is a Socialist Club, a College Democrats Club, and a College Republicans Club. These organizations bring speakers to campus, promote related causes to the UVM community, and provide a link to local and national political organizations.

Gay Tolerance

UVM is a tolerant place where people of all sexual orientations are accepted—and rightly so, since Vermont was the first state to have implemented Civil Unions, and is reputed for being a progressive, liberal place.

Minority Clubs

ALANA (African, Latinos/as, Asian, and Native Americans)

Students Speak Out On...
Diversity

> "It is not racially diverse, I can tell you that. That is the one thing I really don't like about UVM, but then Vermont is not racially diverse either. However, UVM is really diverse in almost every other way."

Q "The campus **isn't racially diverse at all**. There are very few minorities present, and white is definitely the dominant population, which kind of sucks. While there is this lack of racial diversity, there is diversity in other areas. People are very liberal and there is a large, and visible, gay and lesbian community."

Q "**UVM is not very diverse.** There are only four percent of us non-white students in the entire school, which is like 400, but that includes faculty and international students. Those four percent of us are pretty tight though."

Q "Campus is quite diverse, with **many students from overseas** and many other students from all over the country."

Q "Not at all, **well just a little**, but it is pretty shocking to see so many white people everywhere."

Q "There is **definitely a lack of diversity** on campus, and in Vermont in general. Maybe that's part of the reason everyone is required to take a Race and Ethnicity class and a Non-European Cultures class."

Q "It's extremely **diverse in thought, tolerance, ideas, intellectually**, etc., but not at all diverse in race and ethnicity, but we are trying [re: UVM's relationship with Christopher Columbus High School]."

Q "It's not as culturally diverse as it could be, but there are students representing many ethnic backgrounds, and about fifty different countries. The diversity that is here stems from peoples' **different upbringings and thoughts**. You will get into some great conversations at UVM. It is a very liberal place."

Q "UVM, like Vermont, has a fairly homogenous population. Ethnically, a lot of white faces are in every classroom, and foreign students are a novelty. Diversity of sexual orientation is perhaps more prominent, not surprising given the liberal nature of the state. There are some **active organizations supporting diversity** though—ALANA as well as LGBTA."

Q "Diverse? Hardly. This school is mostly populated by **preppy-white-rich-kids**, and then there are the hippies."

The College Prowler Take On...
Diversity

Racial diversity is an area where most UVM students agree there is a need for improvement. Those surveyed commented that the lack of diversity is something many students particularly dislike about UVM. In spite of this, many of these same students also commented on their awareness of the university's diversity with respect to progressiveness and individual thought, as well as the strong presence of the gay community. It is important to remember that diversity is not limited to the color of skin one has. Religious, sexual, political, and racial diversity are important to a diverse community. Unfortunately, here at UVM, although we may have three out of four, that is not good enough. The school is actively pursuing expanding the ethnic and racial diversity here on campus.

While UVM is very diverse in bringing together people with different ideas and unique thoughts, it simply does not have a large flow of minority students. UVM does tend to fare better than the entire state of Vermont, however, which is one of the least diverse states in the nation. In addition, UVM's students are notoriously open minded and not sheltered—much like the Burlington community. Increased racial diversity would expand these qualities at UVM, and improve the community as a whole.

The College Prowler™ Grade on
Diversity: D

A high grade in Diversity indicates that ethnic minorities and international students have a notable presence on campus and that students of different economic backgrounds, religious beliefs, and sexual preferences are well-represented.

Guys & Girls

The Lowdown On...
Guys & Girls

Women Undergrads:
4,840

Men Undergrads:
3,752

Hookups or Relationships?
A bit of both

Top Three Places to Meet Hotties:
Athletic Center
Library
The three places in the next category

Top Three Places to Hook Up:
Parties
Bars
Clubs

Dress Code:
Nearly anything and everything

Students Speak Out On...
Guys & Girls

> "Everyone is pretty nice and generally laid back. The guys are cute and the girls are pretty nice. You will find your group of friends."

Q "The guys would seem to be either potheads or preppies, if you were to generalize. There're lots of skateboarding, skiing, and snowboarding bums, but they're a pretty accepting lot most of the time. They're also pretty good looking most of the time, although some **can be kind of grungy**—dread locks are all over the place. The girls are pretty nice and accepting as well."

Q "Most people don't dress up for class, and lots (including myself) wake up about twenty minutes before class to throw on a sweater, or sweatshirt, and jeans, and then just go to class. Nobody cares if you want to **dress differently**. I find it to be a really comfortable atmosphere."

Q "Well let's just say that you can find quite a variety of guys, from dreads, to preps, to jocks. So it depends on your type of guy. Personally, I'm into the preps and jocks, and I find them quite hot! **Dating isn't popular** on campus at all; it's mostly just random hookups at parties or something."

Q "For the most part, I would say that UVM has a **pretty attractive campus**. However, it's really cold, so people wear sweaters all the time; that gets pretty lame."

Q "**A lot of cute guys** go to UVM, especially the ones in the frats and on the sports teams."

Q "Perhaps the biggest misconception about UVM's student population is the omnipresence of hippies hugging every tree. They're definitely here, but so are the rest of us. Neither guys nor girls can really be pigeon-holed at UVM. Dreadlocks and crew cuts are equally as likely to be pot heads, active members of clubs and organizations, and friends with one another. We do have a pretty physically active student population, providing for a fairly **fit and attractive crowd**."

Q "There are definitely **a lot of hippie-type people** at UVM, and a lot of guys and girls are all dreadlocked out, but they sport a hefty trust fund to boot. There are a lot of great-looking guys and girls around, especially when the weather gets really nice."

Q "The joke is on the girls . . . the guys are okay, but I have **gorgeous girl friends**. It seems that there are better looking women here, but I have seen some hottie-guys too."

Q "There are the hippies. They are nice, but sometimes a little elitist. I don't really go for the hippy-guys so much. There are definitely some hot guys around though. **People tend to be pretty friendly** in Vermont."

Q "My boyfriend says the girls are decent, and I met him here so I guess the men are good. I know that on my floor alone I made some of my best friendships. **No one is snotty, rude, or judgmental**, and I think that that's the best thing about UVM people. On my recruiting visit for soccer, everyone was so friendly. I didn't hear one bad thing about UVM from the students the entire time that I was here. When I signed to play here I told everyone that 'the people sold the place to me'."

Q "You will find that in general everyone on campus is pretty laid back and down to earth. We all take pride in our school and everyone seems to get along no matter what. We all have common interests and connections, whether it happens to be our common interest in music, or in snowboarding, or in whatever. You will **make friends and acquaintances** in no time at all. There are many hot guys at UVM! Were you interested in girls, too? I mean, there are many attractive people at this university in general."

Q "UVM and Burlington **are eclectic in every aspect**. We have the hippies, the dreadlocks, the crunchies, the preps, the jocks, the Vermonters, the transgenders, the skater-punks, the vegans, the vegetarians, the Green Party members, the off-beats, the artsy ones, the outdoorsy ones . . . you name it, we got it. There is a reason why U.S. News and World Report ranked UVM number one in the category of 'Birkenstock-Wearing, Tree-Hugging, Clove-Smoking Vegetarians.'"

The College Prowler Take On...
Guys & Girls

UVM is, of course, infamous for the "hippie" population, but as the surveyed students expressed, all other types of people are here too. The great thing is there are attractive people from all spectrums—every "genre" of person. Moreover, you are as likely to see a sorority girl raising money for the environment as you are to see a dirty-haired, torn-clothed hippie driving a brand-new SUV. The great thing about the people at UVM is that they break many of the stereotypes people often associate with who a person is. We have students sporting Birkenstocks, students clad in J. Crew garb, students active in government, and students dealing drugs—and any one could be at the top of the class.

It is unanimous that both the guys and the girls are attractive. But if anything is missing, it is the mental or emotional connection between people in their relationships. As you will learn once you go to college, the freedoms allocated to students often result in sexual expressions. Hooking-up and having fun seems to be the trend not only here at UVM, but elsewhere in the country as well. There are certainly people in serious relationships, but many people at UVM want nothing more than a casual relationship. However, friendships between men and women are everywhere at UVM—and rest assured that we have people who are both brilliant and beautiful. Also, don't forget that Vermont is the home of the Civil Union; this is a place where preferences don't have to swing in any particular direction to find company.

The College Prowler™ Grade on
Guys: B

A high grade for Guys indicates that the male population on campus is attractive, smart, friendly, and engaging, and that the school has a decent ratio of guys to girls.

The College Prowler™ Grade on
Girls: B+

A high grade for Girls not only implies that the women on campus are attractive, smart, friendly, and engaging, but also that there is a fair ratio of girls to guys.

Athletics

The Lowdown On...
Athletics

Athletic Division:
Division I

Conference:
America East Conference

Men's Teams:
Basketball
Baseball
Cross Country
Golf
Ice Hockey
Lacrosse
Swimming
Skiing
Soccer
Tennis

Women's Teams:
Basketball
Cross Country
Field Hockey
Ice Hockey
Indoor/Outdoor Track
Lacrosse
Swimming
Skiing
Soccer
Softball
Tennis

Club Sports:
13 (e.g. Cycling, Swimming)

Intramurals:
14 (e.g. Frisbee, Lacrosse)

Athletic Fields
Soccer field, Rugby Field, Redstone Field, Football Field (although there is no team)

Gyms/Facilities
Patrick Gymnasium and Fitness Center, Wright Fitness Center

School Mascot
Catamount

Getting Tickets
(802) 656-4410

Most Popular Sports
Hockey, Basketball

Overlooked Teams
Skiing, Golf, Cycling

Best Place to Take a Walk
The bike path that winds behind the school and golf course.

Males Playing Varsity Sports
196 (6%)

Females Playing Varsity Sports
199 (5%)

Students Speak Out On...
Athletics

> "Sports are very big at UVM, especially basketball and hockey. There are many different sports to choose from to play and to watch."

Q "The **gym has a large pool**, as well as tennis courts, racquetball courts, a hockey rink, a weight room, and a dance room."

Q "**Hockey is big at UVM**. I recommend attending as many hockey games as possible, even if you don't like hockey; the social scene is great."

Q "Certain sports are bigger than others. **Hockey and basketball are pretty big**. IM sports seem fun."

Q "I'm on the crew team and I love it! I was in the volleyball club with my friends and that was pretty fun. Both varsity and IM **sports are really popular.**"

Q "UVM has no football team, but our hockey team is a big deal, and so is our basketball team, and I think the soccer team has done well. One of the things that kind of sucks about UVM is school spirit. We do lack a bit in that department, but it's hard when the school **doesn't really promote varsity sports** that much."

Q "Varsity sports are pretty big, with hockey, basketball, and skiing being the dominant sports. **The IM sports are pretty big** too, with a whole host of teams to play with and sports to play. It's also pretty low key, so it's lots of fun."

Q "Sports aren't that big. I referee some IM sports and play in some other ones. However, they are fun, and it's definitely worthwhile to participate in them. I was a member of varsity swimming for two months, but found it **too difficult to manage my time** with all of my classes."

Q "I think that IM sports are really big and a lot of fun. Club and varsity sports are pretty big, but it **depends on the sport**."

Q "Sports are there. They are not huge, but they are definitely there. It's Vermont, and a lot of **people are more into the outdoors**. Our hockey team is well known, though they didn't perform that well this year. It's pretty fun to go to the games."

Q "I don't really know how big varsity sports are on campus, but **intramural sports are tons of fun**."

Q "Varsity sports are fairly big. I play soccer here and **love the sports-scene**."

Q "I play Ultimate Frisbee, which is a club sport. We play other schools and have about ten tournaments per year. **I love it, love it, love it!**"

Q "UVM tends to attract students of the independent spirit rather than those into school spirit. However, there are plenty of jocks at UVM: Hockey is huge on campus, and is widely supported. UVM Skiing is Division I, second in the entire nation, and the **number one team in the East** (the ski team finished second only to the University of Utah at nationals). Most students don't even know this. That in itself suggests how big (or little) sports are at UVM."

The College Prowler Take On...
Athletics

Some varsity sports are much bigger than others. The Alpine Skiing Team and the Nordic Skiing Team rank among the top in the country, while the football team . . . well . . .we don't have a football team. Basketball made a huge splash this past season because they made it, for the first time, into the NCAA tournament. As far as intramurals go, there are a great number of possibilities. There probably exists an IM sport for every varsity sport—sometimes more. This way, if you don't make the cut for varsity, you always have the opportunity to opt into a club sport. Or in some cases, like the UVM Cycling Team, where there is no varsity possibility, anyone can join and be as competitive as he or she wishes. UVM Cycling recently won the overall Eastern Collegiate Cycling Competition beating out schools like Harvard, Yale, Columbia, Middlebury, and Brown.

While UVM has not typically drawn the best athletes from across the country, its reputation as a competitive Division I school is increasing and starting to bring in more athletes at the top of their game. Where the university excels is in its capacity to appease all levels of athletes from the varsity players to those playing their first game of Frisbee. Moreover, there is something to be said for the surroundings of Vermont—enticing many people to take up more independent sports such as climbing, hiking, or cross-country skiing. Whether the allure is a massive crowd of raging fans and the adrenaline peak of excitement as the clock holds vital seconds, or the tranquility of gliding past a Walden-esque pond in the woods dusted with a spraying of snow, there is likely a sport for anyone who cares to participate in one.

The College Prowler™ Grade on
Athletics: B-

A high grade in Athletics indicates that students have school spirit, that sports programs are respected, that games are well-attended, and that intramurals are a prominent part of student life.

Nightlife

The Lowdown On...
Nightlife

Useful Resources for Nightlife:
Friends and a stroll down Church Street

Primary Areas with Nightlife:
Downtown Burlington

Local Specialties:
Microbreweries like Long Trail or Otter Creek

Cheapest Place to Get a Drink:
Dollar Drafts at What Ales You

Favorite Drinking Games:
Beer Pong
Card Games
Century Club
Quarters
Power Hour

Frats:
See the Greek section!

Club and Bar Prowler: Popular Nightlife Spots!

135 Pearl
(802) 863-2343
135 Pearl St., Burlington

This sleek dance club, one of the few in the Burlington area, attracts a varied crowd that congregate to enjoy one commonality: they all dance well into the night. On the lower floor, New England's hottest DJs spin the latest Euro, Techno, and Club tracks, while the upper level features a cozy lounge area where people can talk and socialize without having to yell. 135 Pearl also has a regular schedule of live music, karaoke, drag shows, and theme nights.

Club Metronome
(802) 865-4563
188 Main St., Burlington

One of the town's largest live music venues, Metronome enjoys a prime downtown location above Nectar's. The scene inside is as trendy as one might expect, featuring a red and orange, central bar area, blue floors and ceilings, a mod lounge area with bright yellow walls interrupted by murals, and a dance floor with state-of-the-art light and sound effects. Some of the more well-known musicians that have played at Metronome are Ben Harper, Eddie From Ohio, and the Black Crowes. Cover charges vary.

Coyote Café
(802) 865-3632
161 Church St., Burlington

This hangout, popular with all of Burlington's students, not just UVM's, has been serving delicious Tex-Mex food since 1992, and its friendly staff go the extra mile making sure its patrons have a good time to go along with their great food. On Fridays, expect the bartenders' margarita specials to be coveted, and menu items like wild mushroom tamales, cilantro-seasoned Gulf shrimp, and steak chipotle add to the escape across the border. Group reservations are suggested.

Halvorson's
(802) 658-0278
161 Church St., Church Street Marketplace, Burlington

On upper Church Street, Halvorson's features an extensive pub menu. This popular gathering place draws large crowds year around; however, it really rocks in the summer, when the seating along the Church Street side comes out, and the rear courtyard opens, creating an open-air scene. However, this option is rarely available to UVM students, being that they are usually gone.

Nectar's

(802) 658-4771
188 Main St., Burlington

Well known as the place where Phish got their start, this classic downtown bar and grill is a favorite with locals and students. The interior offers a cozy environment for a quick lunch or an evening gathering with old friends. The menu features an array of standard bar food; including burgers, hot sandwiches, and great fries. In the evening, bartenders concoct cocktails and serve microbrews, while the booths and barstools fill up with a veritable "who's who" of locals.

Red Square Bar and Grill

(802) 859-8909
136 Church St., Burlington

From the front, this former Italian restaurant appears to be a tiny jazz club. Take a few steps inside, and you'll see that Red Square is a never-ending, music-lovers haven. In the warmer months this popular club takes over the alley next to door, and fills it with more tables and another larger stage. The crowd runs the full gamut from college kids to late thirties. There is either a band or DJ every night.

Rí~Rá

(802) 860-9401
123 Church St., Church Street Marketplace, Burlington

One of the more popular places to visit, Rí~Rá offers all the charm and comfort of a traditional Irish pub—in fact, considering that much of the furniture and even the bar itself were built on the Emerald Isle, this place is a traditional Irish pub. The space is divided into four distinct areas, and each has a different mood: the cozy Cottage with its stone fireplace, the Library (ideal for private parties) with its literary theme, and the unique Victorian Shop and Pub with a myriad of Irish trinkets. Rí~Rá hosts a variety of weekly events, from Premier League viewing parties to live music.

Vermont Pub and Brewery

(802) 865-0500
144 College St., Burlington

The state's first brewery/pub, Vermont Pub and Brewery is the brainchild of Greg and Nancy Noonan, who wanted to create a place where Burlington neighbors could share a love for ales and lagers. The pub, which boasts patio seating, includes a menu that includes burgers, fish & chips, bangers & mash, and shepherd's pie. For those with a taste for something with fewer hops, there's a full menu of scotches.

Waiting Room
(802) 862-3455
156 Saint Paul St.

The Waiting Room is an upscale bistro lounge that takes you into the heart of the New York City atmosphere with its overwhelming amount of black and velvet. The club features live music four nights a week, and its fresh seafood, along with the rest of the menu, is available until midnight on Fridays and Saturdays. The Waiting Room is a favorite of Burlington's older crowd, but still draws its fair share of the college kids looking for cosmopolitans instead of Miller Light. The door often has a line, as the staff likes to keep the place from getting too crowded.

Other Places to Check Out:
Parima 185 Pearl St. (802) 864-7917 or The New England Culinary Institute – 25 Church St. (802) 862-6324 – for worldly beer and liqueurs, and fine wine.

What to Do if You're Not 21:
Cafés and/or Restaurants, House/dorm room parties, Higher Ground – 1 Main Winooski (802) 654-8888, Montreal.

Students Speak Out On...
Nightlife

> "Bars and clubs are really awesome in Burlington. A really good club is Nectar's. For a small city like Burlington, you will be surprised how much there is to do here."

- "**A great concert venue** within walking distance from campus is Higher Ground (www.highergroundmusic.com for show listings); a lot of students go there for a fun night of music and dancing!"

- "Church Street is a closed-off street where there are **tons of shops**, stores, restaurants, a mall, some bars, and other such things, and it is only a few blocks from the lakefront."

- "**There are great clubs here**, like the Metronome (new age music), Nectars (live jazz and rock music), Rira (an Irish pub, popular with the older crowd), Rasputin's (for the eighteen to twenty-five crowd), Red Square (a laid back place), What Ales You (a great place for large groups of people), and RJ's (a sit-down place with great wings)."

- "Parties can either be of the chill, small-gathering style, or of the off-the-hook, 'might as well call the cops and ask them to come over' style. **There seem to be enough** of both to satisfy. I'm not twenty-one so I don't know the bar scene. And I don't know the club scene either."

- "There is an eighteen-and-over club called Millennium in the downtown area, but it kind of sucks. If you want to go to good clubs and bars, and aren't twenty-one, and don't have a fake ID, you're in luck: **Montreal is only about one-and-a-half hours away**, and the drinking age there is only eighteen."

Q "The clubs suck! I'm from New York and there is absolutely no comparison to the New York club scene. I'm sorry, but **I don't enjoy the clubs** in Burlington at all. If we ever want to go to a real good dance club, we head up to Montreal, which is about an hour to an hour-and-a-half away by car, and stay up there for the night."

Q "One of the benefits of going to Montreal is that the drinking age there is eighteen. A lot of undergrads head up there to party. If you do decide to stay in Burlington and are desperate to go to the clubs, you can go to Rasputin's or Millennium, but you have to **get there before 11 p.m.** if you are under twenty-one or they won't let you in."

Q "There are lots of bars and clubs around. Of course, you have more of a choice if you're 21 or older, but there are still places to go for the younger crowd. I was never really into frats but they are **always having parties**."

Q "**House parties are pretty much it** until you're twenty-one, unless you have a fake."

Q "Security is pretty tight at the bars and clubs. Do **be careful about trying to get into bars** if you are under twenty-one. Many of the clubs are eighteen and over, so there is always fun stuff to do."

Q "Bars are a lot of fun over here, and they always have great music. **All sorts of music** are big things here. I've never really been to any clubs, but other people seem to like them."

Q "**If you want to party every night, you can**. If you don't, there is no pressure. Greek life boasts a party scene, as do all the students who like to party either in their dorm rooms, or in their houses in downtown Burlington. But there is a reason Vermont's official state color is green . . ."

The College Prowler Take On...
Nightlife

To compliment the many restaurants in the Burlington area, there are a number of bars ranging from a relaxed atmosphere to loud music, and dancing. Turning twenty-one offers many more options; many students are ready for a change of scenery after a couple years of parties and dorm rooms, and welcome the bar scene. There are a number of bars and nightspots for under agers, including Vermont Pub & Brewery, Rasputin's, Club Metronome, and Higher Ground (Burlington's biggest venue for an assortment of music). Montreal is also about two hours away for those looking to go to some clubs and stay overnight. Although Burlington isn't the party Mecca, there are enough venues to keep a student busy, and enough variety to provide everything from a little-city feel to the style of New York City.

Parties on campus, if they occur, tend to be no more than a dozen or so people due to noise regulations and enforcements. The bigger parties happen off campus, usually in frat houses or the like. However, Burlington recently passed a new, stricter, noise ordinance. Drinking and partying are present, but students at UVM have to be cautious and less rowdy since university and city police are quick to hand out liquor violations and noise offenses, which can result in criminal prosecution. If you want to party constantly, or consistently, you may want to look at a bigger state school. Although we like to have a good time here at UVM, it can be difficult with The Man keeping us down. However, once you turn twenty-one, there are a lot more places to go to relax.

The College Prowler™ Grade on
Nightlife: B

A high grade in Nightlife indicates that there are many bars and clubs in the area that are easily accessible and affordable. Other determining factors include the number of options for the under-21 crowd and the prevalence of house parties.

Greek Life

The Lowdown On...
Greek Life

Number of Fraternities:
10

Number of Sororities:
5

Percent of Undergrad Men in Fraternities:
3%

Percent of Undergrad Women in Sororities:
2%

Fraternities on Campus:
Alpha Gamma Rho
Phi Delta Theta
Phi Gamma Delta
Lamda Iota
Delta Psi
Sigma Phi
Alpha Epsilon Pi
Sigma Phi Society
Sigma Phi Epsilon
Pi Kappa Alpha

Sororities on Campus:
Alpha Chi Omega
Alpha Delta Pi
Delta Delta Delta
Kappa Alpha Theta
Pi Beta Phi

Other Greek Organizations:
Greek Council
Greek Peer Advisors
Interfraternity Council

Students Speak Out On...
Greek Life

"Greek life doesn't dominate the social scene at all. If you want to join a sorority or fraternity, you can do so, but there aren't a huge number of them."

Q "The **frat scene is definitely bigger** then the sorority scene."

Q "If you make friends with people who aren't in fraternities or sororities, and live off campus, you'll still have plenty of **great opportunities to party**. Also, if you play a sport, you can count on knowing about plenty of parties."

Q "Greek life is only about ten percent of the school. The **Greeks do supply a lot of the parties** on the weekends, but you definitely don't have to be a part of Greek life in order to fit in; everyone finds their niche."

Q "I am a part of the Greek life on campus. I am a sister in Alpha Delta Pi, a small and selective sorority that exists all over the nation. **Greek life is only five percent of the campus** (that's about 500 kids), but the party scene is dominated by Greeks, at least for me. Were you to join, it would make the campus much smaller—the Greek community rocks!"

Q "Thank God it does not dominate social life, **tends to attract a specific type**. Greek life offers a great sense of community and partying, but only for the five percent of the students of the University of Vermont who actually take part in it."

Q "I am in a sorority and it definitely does not dominate the social scene, but it's something that is **definitely fun to get involved with**."

Q "Greek life is a big thing at UVM, but if you don't choose to be a part of it, there are plenty of other ways to have a good time. I find that Greek life at UVM **doesn't dominate the social scene**, but it gives UVM a good party atmosphere."

Q "I have never gone to a fraternity party, but I've heard they're a good time. If you want to be involved in Greek life, **they have it here**, but it doesn't dominate the social scene. I never had any problems finding something else to do."

Q "I don't know much about the Greek life on campus. I don't really care for it. They definitely do not dominate the social scene. I know they **throw some good parties** though."

Q "Some people are involved with Greek life, but I have many friends who have never been to a frat party. **The sororities never have parties**."

Q "Greek life does exist on this campus, but it is not in any way the only form of social activity. If you want to go to a frat party on the weekends, you'll always be able to find one. However, if that's not your scene, there's **always something else to do**."

The College Prowler Take On...
Greek Life

The people who join Greek life usually want to join, and so they are likely to enjoy it; the ninety-five percent who do not belong to Greek organizations, though, do not miss a beat on anything happening. It is one of those things that most students agree is only there if you want it to be. There is not huge pressure to join a fraternity or sorority, and there is not a high demand for recruits, simply because the presence is not that large. If you want to be a frat boy or a sorority girl, you can, but there will not be as much focus or support as there may be at other universities. Regardless of this, however, by pledging you will still become a member of the house, and hopefully make life-long friends.

This said, you don't have to join a house to make life-long friends. Many students bond with the other people on their floor freshman year, and stay in contact for the remaining three. The Greek life does not dominate the social scene here at UVM. Unlike huge universities with big Greek presence, you do not need to join a fraternity or sorority to do fun things, or be accepted. In fact, there are many chapters that are not present at UVM, and the same opportunities are available to those who do not belong to any Greek house. Most people at UVM do not join or belong to the Greek system, so join if you want to, and don't sweat it if you don't.

The College Prowler™ Grade on
Greek Life: B-

A high grade in Greek Life indicates that sororities and fraternities are not only present, but also active on campus. Other determining factors include the variety of houses available and the respect the Greek community receives from the rest of the campus.

Drug Scene

The Lowdown On...
Drug Scene

Most Prevalent Drugs on Campus:
Alcohol
Marijuana

Liquor-Related Violations:
369

Drug-Related Violations
194

Drug Counseling Programs
Alcohol and Drug Services

Students Speak Out On...
Drug Scene

> "If you want to avoid drugs and drinking, and can't stand people who choose to use them, you should live in a substance-free dorm, or on a substance-free floor."

Q "UVM definitely has a reputation for being strict. It is really **easy to get away with smoking and drinking** in the dorms, especially if you're quiet. A cop is not allowed to enter your room without your consent unless he or she has a reason for doing, so that saves a lot of people!"

Q "A lot of pot everywhere you go. Although you will certainly find those students who do not smoke at all, there are those who smoke so much it will shock you. I smelled it on my floor probably three times a week. But if it doesn't bother you, then it's no big deal at all. Everyone's really **polite about that kind of stuff**, so if you don't want to do it, that's cool. No one will hassle you. Or, if you're into that, they'll always be inviting you to their room to smoke."

Q "**There is pot just about everywhere**. If you want to find some, it's pretty readily available, except when there is a lull in the market, probably the result of a drug bust or something. Substances come around in waves, so there are rarely other given drugs around, except maybe cocaine."

Q "The **kids here are chill**. They just hang around, drink some beers, smoke some pot, and have a good time. While some people choose to do other drugs, hardcore drugs really don't enjoy a popular status at UVM. I came from a school where frat parties consisted of kids shooting up and sniffing crack for fun. I had to get away from that kind of atmosphere."

Q "There is a lot of weed on campus, UVM is well known for it. But if you're not into that kind of thing, don't worry about it. **Not everyone does it**. There are plenty of people at UVM that are not pot heads, trust me."

Q "I heard that the administration is trying to crack down on the pot smoking, but I would say that **it's easier to get drugs** than to get alcohol if you're under twenty-one. Frat parties have alcohol though."

Q "It's Vermont, what do you expect? **Reefer-madness.** Vermont is notorious for "good" marijuana; UVM attracts a lot of the neo-hippies for this very reason."

Q "**Marijuana is used** rabidly and marginalizes many of the individuals who are at UVM for the actual education, not the marijuana. President Fogel is in the midst of changing UVM back to being a public flagship university."

Q "Pot is smoked by a lot of students. Other drugs are around; mushrooms and LSD come in waves. **You can definitely avoid the drug scene** if you choose to do so, or you can be a part of it. It's up to you. If it's something that you are not into, people are very understanding. My advice to you is this: don't go too nuts your first year of college. Often, you will want to try new things because you will have this awesome, new-found freedom, but think about your choices when it comes to harder drugs, or you will most likely regret it later."

The College Prowler Take On...
Drug Scene

As with any college campus, there will be drugs and alcohol, and there will be students who use either, both, or none. And that pretty much sums up UVM as well. Marijuana is the most prevalent illegal substance, along with alcohol (which is illegal to those under 21). Like many students say though, how much you choose to partake is up to you. There are risks involved with drugs and alcohol, and you should be conscious of them before you make a decision. But keep in mind, this is Vermont, and it is a very liberal state. Pot is very common not only here, but in the surrounding Burlington community. It is just important to remember that regardless of whether you engage in drugs and alcohol or not, that you learn to balance your work with your play. Your first priority in going to school is going to school. Many students take college as a playground and ignore their responsibilities and their studies. But if all you do is work, you will have a miserable time at UVM. Just remember to do both, and you will have a great time.

UVM was the longstanding host to the 420 Festival—a massive gathering of students, professors, and community members in support of legalizing marijuana. Perhaps the only significant school spirit event of the year, 420 took place on April 20, at 4:20 p.m. on the lawn outside the library. Pot smokers would light up in unison and peacefully protest the laws against the drug, under the watchful eye of police and administrators. After 2001, the gathering was ousted by huge police presence all over campus, and the threat of prosecution for possession of marijuana should students chose to "light up" in public. UVM has started Spring Fest in place of 420, a day of concerts and promotional give-aways. The change has not been well received by many veterans of the festival, but over time, Spring Fest will probably become the new anticipated tradition. To sum up drugs at UVM, there are definitely drugs here, but if you never want to come in contact with them, you will likely have your wish; if you're looking for them, you'll find them.

The College Prowler™ Grade on
Drug Scene: C+

A high grade in the Drug Scene indicates that drugs are not a noticeable part of campus life; drug use is not visible, and no pressure to use them seems to exist.

Campus Strictness

The Lowdown On...
Campus Strictness

What Are You Most Likely to Get Caught Doing on Campus?
- Drinking underage
- Smoking pot

Students Speak Out On...
Campus Strictness

> "Campus police are Vermont State Police, so you need to be careful about what you do."

Q "UVM often has security guards roaming the halls of campus facilities during the night on all days of the week, but even more so on the weekends. There are also many **police cars that drive around** campus on the weekends, when students are likely to be out."

Q "Most of the officers I've encountered have been **very nice**, though I do know students who've had problems with them."

Q "They are **very strict**—it's obnoxious."

Q "Campus police suck. They have **no regard for students' rights** and really come down hard on the students. The detoxification program is even worse. The best thing to do is not to be stupid. Don't ever walk home alone, and don't party in the dorms, ever. It's stupid and you will get caught."

Q "The University is extremely strict. **Three strikes and you are out**."

Q "The UVM police are very strict about drinking in the dorms if you're under age. If you're over twenty-one, you can drink in the dorms though. There is basically **no tolerance for drugs**, and it seems to be a constant topic of debate."

Q "A lot of people smoke in their rooms. If that's not for you, **request a roommate who does not smoke**. It will make your life easier!""

Q "**Campus police are strict**, but you can definitely get away with stuff; everyone does."

The College Prowler Take On...
Campus Strictness

The campus-wide implementation of strictness leaves some students aggravated and feeling as though their rights are being violated. Other students, meanwhile, like the added feeling of security provided by increased police presence and firmness. Whatever the belief, common sense will keep you out of trouble, and prevent you from having to answer to the law.

As aforementioned, campus police are stricter than they used to be. They are more lenient to alcohol offenses than they are marijuana charges, but if you're irresponsible, or unlucky, you are asking for trouble. As it stands, charges for possession of pot endangers your chances of obtaining, or continuing to receive, federal student aid including loans and grants—a line that many people can't afford to cross.

The College Prowler™ Grade on Campus Strictness: D+

A high Campus Strictness grade implies an overall lenient atmosphere; police and RAs are fairly tolerant, and the administration's rules are flexible.

Parking

The Lowdown On...
Parking

Student Parking Lot?
Yes

Freshmen Allowed to Park?
Only with permission

Approximate Parking Permit Cost:
$140 per year

Best Place to Find a Parking Spot:
Gutterson (albeit very far from everything)

Good Luck Getting a Parking Spot Here:
Anywhere that is not Gutterson, particularly Redstone

Common Parking Tickets:
Any car without a parking permit will get a first offense warning, upon a second offense there is a $30 or $50 ticket.

Students Speak Out On...
Parking

"**The parking scene sucks!** Parking on campus is almost impossible, and they ticket like mad. But the campus is a pretty easy place to get around, so if you live on, or near, campus, you can easily walk or ride your bike to class."

Q "At UVM, you cannot have a car on campus as a first-year student. You really **don't need one** though."

Q "Freshmen are not allowed to have cars. There is limited space for parking on campus, so they reserve it for the upperclassmen. If you don't have a parking permit, be prepared to pay parking tickets. They are expensive, but they are issued by UVM, not Burlington, so few people take them seriously. After only three tickets **they will tow your car!**"

Q "**Parking is pretty bad**. Freshmen are not allowed to bring cars to school, so that rules that out for you unless you have a job which requires a certain amount of hours. That allows you to get a parking permit from parking services."

Q "**Parking is horrible**. And on top of that, no freshman is allowed to have a car."

Q "You can only have a car on campus if you are a sophomore, and even then it is **determined by lottery** (whether or not you get a space at all)."

Q "I don't know who gets to park on Main Campus during the day—it is **certainly not me**."

Q "On East Campus parking is good, on Redstone parking is bad, off campus there is **some street parking** which is first-come first-serve. You can't have a car during your freshman year."

Q "Freshmen can't have cars on campus, and parking has always been a problem. **Sophomores, juniors and seniors can park** by the hockey rink, but usually have to catch a shuttle to class."

Q "It is very hard to park, and it is **hard to find a spot in town** too, they ticket like crazy here."

Did You Know?

The Morgan Horse Farm in Weybridge, VT was established in 1878 when Joseph Battell of Middlebury gathered the first-ever volume of the Morgan Horse Registry and built the farm. Morgan Horses, which date back 1789, are extremely intelligent and versatile horses; the Morgan Horse is also Vermont's State Animal.

The College Prowler Take On...
Parking

Survey Says: Parking is not fun! As UVM continues to grow, so do the number of people wishing to have a car on campus. Regardless, students agree that parking is not ideal in this pedestrian town, and even more difficult on campus. Seldom do students find a parking space on their first loop though the lot, and often they must park extremely far away from their dorm. On top of that, spaces are cramped and get even tighter when it snows. Students' overwhelming advice is to leave the car at home unless utterly necessary.

Parking at UVM is not likely to be resolved any time soon. It is a quandary that plagues the entire student body—or at least those with wheels. Parking passes for upperclassmen living on campus are doled out through a lottery system, and then those students who receive notification of having been granted a parking space can purchase a pass. They charge up to $143 per year for a parking permit, but then you're not guaranteed a space even within site of your dorm. The parking lots are overly crowded and not lined well, and many students are inconsiderate with these conditions. The tickets they give for parking "out of your zone" are outrageous: $30 for the first offense, $50 for the second, and tow your car after the third offense (at your expense, of course). Only bring your car if you absolutely must, or if you know you'll use it all the time. The final complaint: First-year students are not allowed a parking permit. As far as driving to class, definitely don't bother; there is certainly nowhere near the academic buildings to park, even for guests.

The College Prowler™ Grade on
Parking: D+

A high grade in this section indicates that parking is both available and affordable, and that parking enforcement isn't overly severe.

Transportation

The Lowdown On...
Transportation

Ways to Get Around Town
Walking
CATS Shuttle Bus
Bio Diesel Bus
Taxis

Ways to Get Out of Town
Amtrak
For Schedules and Reservations:
(800) 872-7245

For Station Information only:
(802) 879-7298

Vermont Transit
345 Pine St., Burlington
(802) 864-6811

CCTA Bus
(802) 864-0211

Lake Champlain Ferries
King St. Dock, Burlington
(802) 864-9804

2901 Ferry Rd., Charlotte
(802) 425-2504

Friends
As in, use your friend's car

Burlington International Airport
(802) 863-1889.
Business Express: (800) 345-3400

Airlines Serving Burlington:
American Airlines, (800) 433-7300, www.americanairlines.com
Continental, (800) 525-0280, www.continental.com
Delta, (800) 221-1212, www.delta-air.com
Northwest, (800) 225-2525, www.nwa.com
JetBlue, (800) 538-2583, www.jetblue.com
United, (800) 241-6522, www.united.com
US Airways, (800) 428-4322, www.usairways.com

Students Speak Out On...
Transportation

> "There are free shuttle buses that go all over campus and there are also buses that go both downtown, and to the mall, which is about two miles away."

Q "It's very convenient. Public **transportation is very accessible** and reasonably priced. It's a very good system."

Q "**Public transportation is convenient**. There are shuttles that will take you into Burlington for free after 6 p.m. every night, but they come around once every half-hour, which is kind of a pain. Walking is probably the most popular mode of transportation for those who don't have a car."

Q "Transportation is great, but I **walk everywhere**. There are buses that run periodically, and on schedule."

Q "Public transportation is good. The UVM shuttle takes you from one campus to another. You'll love taking it in the winters, but be warned: depending on the time of day, **the bus could be too packed**, and you won't be able to get on, and so you'll have to wait a few more minutes for the next bus. To go downtown (where Church Street is located), you could take a taxi, you could walk (depending on how far you are and how motivated you are), or you could catch the CCT, which is the public bus service. It's free for college students."

Q "**Public transportation is not hard to use** at all. We also have campus buses that will take you downtown for free, and it only costs $2 to take the public bus service to the airport. The airport is about ten minutes away."

Q "**There are free shuttles** that run all over campus, and even travel downtown. Taxi fare is also cheap, usually costing $5-$10. The public bus system is decent from what I've heard, but you don't really need to use it."

Q "UVM buses are not bad; they run every fifteen minutes. I have never used the public transportation system, as I have always simply **depended on my friends** for their cars."

Q "It is **easiest for me to walk**, or ride my bike. I hate to drive, and I think that the town is such that I don't have to a lot, but I don't use buses a lot."

The College Prowler Take On...
Transportation

Public transportation is hit or miss, but usually easy and reliable. On campus, it is plentiful and easy, but downtown it is a little bit harder to secure a ride. The plus is UVM is just a stones throw from downtown Burlington, and the city itself is actually relatively small. So, while there is public bus transportation, sometimes it's quicker just to walk. If you know the schedule well enough, though, you're not likely to run into too many problems. When you live in an isolated area like Burlington, walking is favorable. However, when the winter months come, it may be unbearable to venture downtown on foot.

Burlington is certainly small enough that every corner of it can be reached by foot. Because of this, most students either do not utilize, or do not need, public transportation. For those that do, however, or for those who want it, it is present. The buses in Burlington are inexpensive, and for the most part, convenient. The ways out of town—either via bus, train or plane—are also relatively reasonably priced and available to all who want it. Ultimately, it is a convenient and stress free way to take the hassle out of parking, or worrying about a car, when driving in a city that is filled with pedestrians.

The College Prowler™ Grade on
Transportation: B+

A high grade for Transportation indicates that campus buses, public buses, cabs, and rental cars are readily-available and affordable. Other determining factors include proximity to an airport and the necessity of transportation.

Weather

The Lowdown On...
Weather

Average Temperature
Fall: 48 °F
Winter: 19 °F
Spring: 44 °F
Summer: 70 °F

Average Precipitation
Fall: 3.37 in.
Winter: 2.04 in.
Spring: 2.86 in.
Summer: 3.77 in.

Did You Know?

Vermont is the producer of world famous **maple syrup**.

Students Speak Out On...
Weather

> "If you like long winters with lots of snow, you'll like Vermont. Almost everyone at this school seems to love skiing, so that's one advantage of getting so much snow. The fall always brings pretty foliage."

Q "They say that Vermont has five seasons: snow, more snow, too much snow, mud, and then summer. Having lived in Vermont for my entire life, I'm used to it. A quick example of the weather: last weekend we had a little snow, and today it was eighty degrees and I got sunburned. So the **weather is quite unpredictable**."

Q "Burlington is the most beautiful place in the United States during the spring. The weather is always changing, but it does get pretty cold in the winter, and there are a fair number of cloudy days. But the **fall is absolutely amazing**, and spring in Vermont is the best! Winter is incredible, but I'm a snow bum."

Q "The weather is unpredictable, so it's best to **prepare for freezing-cold** temperatures in the range of negative ten to negative twenty-five degrees. And wind and precipitation, don't forget about those factors."

Q "Let's just say that the weather is cold. In the winter it can get below zero, so bring lots of warm clothing and sweaters. It also gets windy, but don't let the weather fool you; it's a lot of fun here. But for example, in April we had a heat stroke and it was **ninety degrees all week**."

Q "It's pretty much really cold in the winter. **We get a ton of snow,** which is really good if you like to ski. Otherwise, it seems to rain a lot, or to be cloudy a lot, but there are some beautiful days in the spring when it is perfect for a trip down to Lake Champlain."

Q "I love Vermont because it is one of the few states in the country that has four distinct seasons. Moreover, each of these seasons is **equally beautiful**. The weather is extremely capricious and fickle, and scares away a lot of first-year students from returning for their sophomore year. Bring clothing for every season. Do not plan on wearing your spring clothes in spring—you'll still be wearing your winter clothes consistently throughout April and May."

The College Prowler Take On...
Weather

The weather here is amazing . . . wait, no, it's terrible . . . er, actually, the weather in Vermont is anything but predictable. That's why most Vermonters will give you the age-old adage, "If you don't like the weather, wait five minutes." This little quip isn't too far from the truth, though, so be prepared for anything. This past year gave us two extremes: the summer with new record-breaking highs, while winter blessed us with temperatures dipping below zero degrees for close to two months. This is a state where April showers often come in May, and winter usually appears, not in late December, but anywhere between October and Thanksgiving. As far as clothes go, come prepared. Vermont can have simply wonderful weather, but it can also quickly turn dismal. Think of living in a place with temperatures ranging from fifteen degrees below zero, not including wind chill, and up to the nineties, not accounting for humidity. And don't forget to bring some sort of boot/shoe for snow!

Some students love it, some of them hate it, but in actuality it is the whole of this love-hate relationship that describes student's feelings about the weather. People who live to ski are thrilled that Vermont has some of the best skiing in the East, with what are usually long and snowy winters. Those who are into hiking appreciate the colorful splashes of leaves in the autumn, or the vibrant flowers in spring. And for the rest who enjoy water sports like swimming or kayaking, Vermont also has sweltering hot and humid summers. There is indeed a little taste of everything for everybody.

The College Prowler™ Grade on
Weather: C-

A high Weather grade designates that temperatures are mild and rarely reach extremes, that the campus tends to be sunny rather than rainy, and that weather is fairly consistent rather than unpredictable.

UNIVERSITY OF VERMONT
Report Card Summary

ACADEMICS	B-
LOCAL ATMOSPHERE	A-
SAFETY AND SECURITY	A-
COMPUTERS	B+
FACILITIES	B+
CAMPUS DINING	B+
OFF-CAMPUS DINING	A-
CAMPUS HOUSING	B
OFF-CAMPUS HOUSING	B
DIVERSITY	D
GUYS	B
GIRLS	B+
ATHLETICS	B-
NIGHTLIFE	B
GREEK LIFE	B-
DRUG SCENE	C+
CAMPUS STRICTNESS	D+
PARKING	D+
TRANSPORTATION	B+
WEATHER	C-

Overall Experience

Students Speak Out On...
Overall Experience

"Overall, I think that UVM is a blast. There are lots of people, lots of things to do, the mountains are so pretty, and the lake is so beautiful. It's a pretty campus, the people are nice, and the academics are good. I say go for it."

Q "I love UVM. The quality of people at this school is amazing. As with any school, I would recommend **getting involved in the school community**. It makes such a difference in your overall experience. I am a member of ADPI, and the Greek community as a whole. I have also been a columnist for the school newspaper, and I just completed a work-study job this year. Without these activities, I would have never met all the people that I met."

Q "**UVM is a lot of fun** and has great academics. There is always something to do and somewhere to go to just get away if you need to for a while. Being from the area myself, I sometimes get bored with the town, but with Montreal being only an hour away there is always a whole new place to explore, and in which to party. I highly recommend it, and perhaps I'll see you on campus."

Q "I transferred here from UConn and **I couldn't be happier**, I don't wish I was anywhere else."

Q "There's **plenty of really fun stuff** to do around Burlington—cool bars, restaurants, Church Street, and outdoors stuff like hiking and camping. Burlington's right on beautiful Lake Champlain . . . The Adirondacks and the Green Mountains are really close to Burlington . . . Montreal is only about an hour-and-a-half away (the drinking age in Montreal is 18)—very crazy and very fun."

Q "I love it and I fit right in with my school. You really have to be **very liberal**, very open to new things, very open to homosexuality, and very willing to be screwed over by the system, although everything will turn out fine in the end."

Q "I do wish that I was not at UVM. I wish that I would have **stayed in New York**, preferably in the city. Like I said before, I'm from New York, a little outside the city, and I just miss the city life."

Q "Ambivalence. I love New England and Vermont (especially Burlington), and **I love to ski**, which is why I came to UVM. I have had an extremely positive experience academically and socially . . . although, I'm looking forward to meeting people more on my "wavelength" as I progress each semester."

Q "I might be happier at a bigger school, where there are probably more down-to-earth people, as opposed to all of the **stereotypical, superficial hippie** UVM people you would find here. I might be a tad bit unhappy about where I am though."

Q "I chose UVM instead of a particularly well-respected liberal arts college in New England. I still question my choice, but am confident that my second year at UVM will affirm the decision I made. This city is what has kept me at UVM; **I will never find another Burlington . . . anywhere**."

Q "College was a huge decision for me. I wanted the best total college package and **I can't believe how lucky I am** to have found it here at UVM. My father and I visited over twenty schools nationwide and I chose UVM over all of them. You can walk downtown in Burlington wearing sweatpants or a prom dress, and no one will think twice about it."

The College Prowler Take On...
Overall Experience

Students are in agreement that the University of Vermont is a remarkable place to go to school. The refreshing environment and lovely surroundings meld well with the progressive, laidback city of Burlington. One particular area students wished to see change is an increase in the amount of racial diversity at UVM. Perhaps the coming years will bring a more diverse application pool, allowing students to learn in a varied and culturally aware environment. And, while less consequential factors such as parking or Greek life were neither praised nor abhorred, the most important aspects of college, such as academics, atmosphere, and housing, consistently achieved superior rankings according to the students.

Compared with most other state universities, the University of Vermont offers a very competitive educational experience in an unbeatable setting. It is like an epicenter—within a day's drive of New York, Boston, the Atlantic Ocean, and Canada. The University of Vermont houses provocative and diverse thoughts, mixed with a dedicated student body, and the additional flair of Burlington. The verdict is out: UVM is a beautiful school with a rigorous academic curriculum, mixed together in a place that people come to enjoy and, surely, continue to love.

The Inside Scoop

The Lowdown On...
The Inside Scoop

Tips to Succeed at UVM
- Major in something you are going to enjoy.
- Set aside time for friends.
- Have fun learning.
- Make an effort to get involved.
- Introduce yourself to professors—put a face with the name.

Finding a Job or Internship

The Lowdown On...
Finding a Job or Internship

It is best to check in with the career center. They can help you write a resume and network with a variety of people, places, and fields.

Career Center Resources and Services:
www.uvm.edu/~career
(802) 656-3450

Graduates Entering Job Market
6 Months After Graduation: 72%
1 Year After Graduation: 87%

Firms That Hire Graduates
Fletcher Allen Health Care, State of Vermont, IBM, Price Waterhouse Coopers, American Express, Burton Snowboards, Mass General Hospital, University of Vermont, U. S. Government, Massachusetts General Hospital, Dufresne-Henry, Americorps, Allscripts Healthcare, Northeastern family Institute, Ben & Jerry's, Beth Israel Deaconess Medical Ctr, Brigham & Women's Hospital, Children's Hospital(Boston), Dana farber Cancer Institute, Harvard University, Husky Injection Molding, IDX, John Hancock, NY Presbyterian Hospital, ORC

It is best to check in with the career center. They can help you write a resume and network with a variety of people, places, and fields.

Career Center Resources and Services:

www.uvm.edu/~career

(802) 656-3450

Alumni

The Lowdown On...
Alumni

Website:
alumni.uvm.edu

Email:
alumni@uvm.edu

Office:
The University of Vermont Development and Alumni Relations
Grasse Mount Building
411 Main St.
Burlington, VT 05401

Hours
8 a.m. - 5 p.m. (EST)

Phone
(802) 656-201
Toll Free: (888) 458-8691
Fax: (802) 656-8678

Services Available
Lifetime e-mail forwarding

Major Alumni Events
The alumni office hosts an annual reunion and the Homecoming & Family Weekend.

Alumni Publications

<u>Vermont Quarterly</u> – The UVM magazine for alumni, parents & friends

<u>The View</u> – The electronic magazine for the UVM campus community

Famous Alumni

John Dewey (1879) – Renowned philosopher and educator

Jody Williams ('72) – Won the 1997 Nobel Peace Prize for her continuing efforts to ban landmines worldwide

Libby Smith ('02) – Professional golfer

Student Organizations

The Lowdown On...
Student Organizations

Agriculture and Life Sciences:
Alpha Zeta Fraternity
Collegiate 4-H
Common Ground
CREAM
Dairy Club
Dressage Team
Equestrian Team
EQUUS
Horse Club
Horticulture Club
Pre-vet Club://alumni.uvm.edu

Engineering-Mathematics
American Society of Civil Engineers
American Society for Engineering Management
American Society of Mechanical Engineers
L/L Engineering & Mathematics Program
Mathematical Association of America
Society of Automotive Engineers
Society of Women Engineers
Tau Beta Pi
Upsilon Pi Epsilon

For Diversity

Alianza Latina
Asian American Student Union
Catholic Student Association
Chabad Jewish Student Organization
Chinese Student Association
Free To Be: GLBTA
Hillel
Inter-Varsity Christian Fellowship
Spurgeon Foundation Campus Ministries
Students for Global Peace and Justice
Students Organizing Against Racism
Students Political Awareness and Responsibility Collective (SPARC)
Vermont Pagans
Volunteers In Action (VIA)
HIV/AIDS Task Force
Women Helping Battered Women
Women Organizing for Radical Change
World Club (The Saladbowl)

The Best & The Worst

The Ten BEST Things About UVM:

1. The weather (If you are a skier or outdoors person)
2. Spectacular scenery
3. Laidback people
4. Outstanding professors
5. Progressive student body
6. Safe and thriving city locale
7. Access to Montreal, Canada
8. An assorted slew of music, art, and food
9. Easy access to the great outdoors
10. Great skiing nearby

The Ten **WORST** Things About UVM:

1. The weather (Cold winters and unpredictability)
2. Parking (or lack thereof)
3. Strict policies
4. 6 a.m. registration
5. Few on-campus housing alternatives to dorm rooms
6. Lack of school spirit
7. Students can be cliquey - leftover high school mentality
8. Lacking diversity
9. All those fun things to do might distract from schoolwork
10. All that schoolwork might distract from the fun things to do

Visiting UVM

The Lowdown On...
Visiting UVM

Hotel Information

Best Western
1076 Williston Rd., S. Burlington
(800) 371-1125

Clarion Hotel
1117 Williston Rd., S. Burlington
(800) 252-7466

Comfort Inn
1285 Williston Rd., S. Burlington
(800) 228-5150

Hawthorn Suites
401 Dorset St., S. Burlington
(800) 527-1133

Holiday Inn
1068 Williston Rd., S. Burlington
(800) 799-6363

Lang House (B&B)
360 Main St., Burlington
(802) 652-2500

→

Sheraton
870 Williston Rd., Burlington
(800) 677-6576

University Inn
5 Dorset St., S. Burlington
(800) 808-4656

Willard Street Inn (B&B)
349 S. Willard St., Burlington
(802) 651-8710]

Wyndham Hotel
60 Battery St., Burlington
(800) 996-3425

Take a Campus Virtual Tour

Go to *www.uvm.edu/about_uvm/online_tours*

To Schedule a Group Information Session or Interview
Contact the Office of Undergraduate Admissions at:
194 S. Prospect St.
Burlington, VT 05401
Phone: (802) 656-3370
e-mail: admissions@uvm.edu

Campus Tours

(Reservations required) Ninety-minute walking tours are led by a student AdvoCat and are offered most weekdays at 10 a.m. and 2 p.m. Make a reservation online or call (802) 656-3370. Reservation cancellations may be made online or by calling the Admissions Office.

Information Sessions

(Reservations required) Forty-five-minute group sessions led by admissions counselors are followed by a ninety-minute, student-led walking tour. They are available Mondays, Fridays, and Saturdays from mid-July through August. Make a reservation online or call (802) 656-3370. Reservation cancellations may be made online or by calling the Admissions Office.

Directions to Campus

Driving from the South
Interstate 87 comes up through New York
Take the Glens Falls exit into Rutland, VT and continue North on Route 7

Driving from the East
Interstate 89 comes right into Burlington.

Driving from the West
Either Interstate 88 across New York State or Interstate 90 through Michigan and then New York will meet in Albany, NY. Continue North on Interstate 87 until the Glens Fall exit, or stay North and take the ferry across Lake Champlain.

Words to Know

Academic Probation – A student can receive this if they fail to keep up with their school's academic minimums. Those who are unable to improve their grades after receiving this warning can possibly face dismissal.

Beer Pong / Beirut – A drinking game with numerous cups of beer arranged in a particular pattern on each side of a table. The goal is to get a ping pong ball into one of the opponent's cups by throwing the ball or hitting it with a paddle. If the ball lands in a cup, the opponent is required to drink the beer.

Bid – An invitation from a fraternity or sorority to pledge their specific house.

Blue Light Phone – Brightly-colored phone posts with a blue light bulb on top. These phones exist for security purposes and are located at various outside locations around most campuses. If a student has an emergency or is feeling endangered, they can pick up one of these phones (free of charge) to connect with campus police or an escort service.

Campus Police – Policemen who are specifically assigned to a given institution. Campus police are not regular city officers; they are employed by the university in a full-time capacity.

Club Sports – A level of sports that falls somewhere between varsity and intramural. If a student is unable to commit to a varsity team but has a lot of passion for athletics, a club sport could be a better, less intense option. If a club sport still requires too much commitment, intramurals often involve no traveling and a lot less time.

Cocaine – An illegal drug. Also known as "coke" or "blow," cocaine often resembles a white crystalline or powdery substance. It is highly addictive and dangerous.

Common Application – An application that students can use to apply to multiple schools.

Course Registration – The time when a student selects what courses they would like for the upcoming quarter or semester. Prior to registration, it is best to have an idea of several back-up courses in case a particular class becomes full. If a course is full, a student can place themselves on the waitlist, although this still does not guarantee entry.

Division Athletics – Athletics range from Division I to Division III. Division IA is the most competitive, while Division III is considered to be the least competitive.

Dorm – Short for dormitory, a dorm is an on-campus housing facility. Dorms can provide a range of options from suite-style rooms to more communal options that include shared bathrooms. Most first-year students live in dorms. Some upperclassmen who wish to stay on campus also choose this option.

Early Action – A way to apply to a school and get an early acceptance response without a binding commitment. This is a system that is becoming less and less available.

Early Decision – An option that students should use only if they are positive that a place is their dream school. If a student applies to a school using the early decision option and is admitted, they are required and bound to attend that university. Admission rates are usually higher with early decision students because the school knows that a student is making them their first choice.

Ecstasy – An illegal drug. Also known as "e" or "x," ecstasy looks like a pill and most resembles an aspirin." Considered a party drug, ecstasy is very dangerous and can be deadly.

Ethernet – An extremely fast internet connection that is usually available in most university-owned residence halls. To use an Ethernet connection properly, a student will need a network card and cable for their computer.

Fake ID – A counterfeit identification card that contains false information. Most commonly, students get fake IDs and change their birthdates so that they appear to be older than 21 (of legal drinking age). Even though it is illegal, many college students have fake IDs in hopes of purchasing alcohol or getting into bars.

Frosh – Slang for "freshmen."

Hazing – Initiation rituals that must be completed for membership into some fraternities or sororities. Numerous universities have outlawed hazing due to its degrading or dangerous requirements.

Sports (IMs) – A popular, and usually free, student activity where students create teams and compete against other groups for fun. These sports vary in competitiveness and can include a range of activities—everything from billiards to water polo. IM sports are a great way to meet people with similar interests.

Keg – Officially called a half barrel, a keg contains roughly 200 12-ounce servings of beer and is often found at college parties.

LSD – An illegal drug. Also known as acid, this hallucinogenic drug most commonly resembles a tab of paper.

Marijuana – An illegal drug. Also known as weed or pot; besides alcohol, marijuana is one of the most commonly-found drugs on campuses across the country.

Major – The focal point of a student's college studies; a specific topic that is studied for a degree. Examples of majors include physics, English, history, computer science, economics, business, and music. Many students decide on a specific major before arriving on campus, while others are simply "undecided" and figure it out later. Those who are extremely interested in two areas can also choose to double major.

Meal Block – The equivalent of one meal. Students on a "meal plan" usually receive a fixed number of meals per week.

Each meal, or "block," can be redeemed at the school's dining facilities in place of cash. More often than not, if a student fails to use their weekly allotment of meal blocks, they will be forfeited.

Minor – An additional focal point in a student's education. Often serving as a compliment or addition to a student's main area of focus, a minor has fewer requirements and prerequisites to fulfill than a major. Minors are not required for graduation from most schools; however some students who want to further explore many different interests choose to have both a major and a minor.

Mushrooms – An illegal drug. Also known as "shrooms," this drug looks like regular mushrooms but are extremely hallucinogenic.

Off-Campus Housing – Housing from a particular landlord or rental group that is not affiliated with the university. Depending on the college, off-campus housing can range from extremely popular to non-existent. Those students who choose to live off campus are typically given more freedom, but they also have to deal with things such as possible subletting scenarios, furniture, and bills. In addition to these factors, rental prices and distance often affect a student's decision to move off campus.

Office Hours – Time that teachers set aside for students who have questions about the coursework. Office hours are a good place for students to go over any problems and to show interest in the subject material.

Pledging – The time after a student has gone through rush, received a bid, and has chosen a particular fraternity or sorority they would like to join. Pledging usually lasts anywhere from one to two semesters. Once the pledging period is complete and a particular student has done everything that is required to become a member, they are considered a brother or sister. If a fraternity or a sorority would decide to "haze" a group of students, these initiation rituals would take place during the pledging period.

Private Institution – A school that does not use taxpayers dollars to help subsidize education costs. Private schools typically cost more than public schools and are usually smaller.

Prof – Slang for "professor."

Public Institution – A school that uses taxpayers dollars to help subsidize education costs. Public schools are often a good value for in-state residents and tend to be larger than most private colleges.

Quarter System (sometimes referred to as the Trimester System) – A type of academic calendar system. In this setup, students take classes for three academic periods. The first quarter usually starts in late September or early October and concludes right before Christmas. The second quarter usually starts around early to mid–January and finishes up around March or April. The last quarter, or "third quarter," usually starts in late March or early April and finishes up in late May or Mid-June. The fourth quarter is summer. The major difference between the quarter system and semester system is that students take more courses but with less coverage.

RA (Resident Assistant) – A student leader who is assigned to a particular floor in a dormitory in order to help to the other students who live there. A RA's duties include ensuring student safety and providing guidance or assistance wherever possible.

Recitation – An extension of a specific course; a "review" session of sorts. Because some classes are so large, recitations offer a setting with fewer students where students can ask questions and get help from professors or TAs in a more personalized environment. As a result, it is common for most large lecture classes to be supplemented with recitations.

Rolling Admissions – A form of admissions. Most commonly found at public institutions, schools with this type of policy continue to accept students throughout the year until their class sizes are met. For example, some schools begin accepting students as early as December and will continue to do so until April or May.

Room and Board – This is typically the combined cost of a university-owned room and a meal plan.

Room Draw/Housing Lottery – A common way to pick on-campus room assignments for the following year. If a student decides to remain in university-owned housing, they are assigned a unique number that, along with seniority, is used to choose their new rooms for the next year.

Rush – The period in which students can meet the brothers and sisters of a particular chapter and find out if a given fraternity or sorority is right for them. Rushing a fraternity or a sorority is not a requirement at any school. The goal of rush is to give students who are serious about pledging a feel for what to expect.

Semester System – The most common type of academic calendar system at college campuses. This setup typically includes two semesters in a given school year. The "fall" semester starts around the end of August or early September and finishes right before winter vacation. The "spring" semester usually starts in mid-January and ends around late April or May.

Student Center/Rec Center/Student Union – A common area on campus that often contains study areas, recreation facilities, and eateries. This building is often a good place to meet up with fellow students and is most commonly used as a hangout. Depending on the school, the student center can have a huge role or a non-existent role in campus life.

Student ID – A university-issued photo ID that serves as a student's key to many different functions within an institution. Some schools require students to show these cards in order to get into dorms, libraries, cafeterias, and other facilities. In addition to storing meal plan information, in some cases, a student ID can actually work as a debit card and allow students to purchase things from bookstores or local shops.

Suite – A type of dorm room. Unlike other places that have communal bathrooms that are shared by the entire floor, a suite has a private bathroom. Suite-style dorm rooms can house anywhere from two to ten students.

TA (Teacher's Assistant) – An undergraduate or grad student who helps in some manner with a specific course. In some cases, a TA will teach a class, assist a professor, grade assignments, or conduct office hours.

Undergraduate – A student who is in the process of studying for their Bachelor (college) degree.

ABOUT THE AUTHOR:

The University of Vermont has thus far lent me an extraordinary experience. Initially, I wanted to attend a small liberal-arts college, but after coming to UVM and settling in, I eventually found myself beyond happiness, despite its large size. For me, everything really started coming together during my sophomore year when I was more familiar with what the school, and professors, had to offer. I got to take more classes that I really wanted to, and my real friendships were solidified. UVM rekindled my love of academics, and I am now looking forward to a possible future in the scholarly circle.

Writing this guidebook has been both a pleasure and an honor. I am currently entering my junior year at the University of Vermont pursuing a double major in English and Religion with a focus on philosophy. As a native Vermonter, I have come to appreciate UVM for the same reasons I love Vermont: its beautiful surroundings, and endless opportunities and activities for those who cannot get enough of the outdoors. Cycling throughout the green mountains and skiing during the winters have both given me unique perspectives on this picturesque state. The University of Vermont has been an invaluable transitioning step toward achieving my goal of competing in cycling, as well as a working force in opening the doors to further study in graduate school. Whatever I end up doing, I know I will be passionate about it, as passion supercedes all other priorities, and in my opinion, provides the building blocks to happiness.

If given the choice, I would not wish to go any other place. Looking back on the people I've met and the opportunities I've seized, the classes I've had, and the places I've gone, I cannot see it any other way. The more I learned the more I grew. I have changed in many different ways since high school, all for the better, and I accredit much of this to the friends I've made, and my personal experience with education, experience, and life. I will never turn back.

Thanks for reading.

Kevyn Jonas Lenfest

KevynLenfest@collegeprowler.com

Notes

Notes

Notes

Notes

Notes

Notes

Notes

Notes

Notes

Notes

Notes

Notes

Notes

Notes

Notes

Notes

Notes

Notes

Need More Help?

Do you have more questions about this school? Can't find a certain statistic? College Prowler is here to help. We are the best source of college information on the planet. We have a network of thousands of students who can get the latest information on any school to you ASAP. E-mail us at *info@collegeprowler.com* with your college-related questions. It's like having an older sibling show you the ropes!

Email Us Your College-Related Questions!

Check out **www.collegeprowler.com** for more details.
1.800.290.2682

Notes

Tell Us What Life Is Really Like At Your School!

Have you ever wanted to let people know what your school is really like? Now's your chance to help millions of high school students choose the right school.

Let your voice be heard and win cash and prizes!

Check out **www.collegeprowler.com** for more info!

Notes

Do You Have What It Takes To Get Admitted?

The College Prowler Road to College Counseling Program is here. An admissions officer will review your candidacy at the school of your choice and create a 12+ page personal admission plan. We rate your credentials with the same criteria used by school admissions committees. We assess your strengths and weaknesses and create a plan of action that makes a difference.

Check out **www.collegeprowler.com** or call 1.800.290.2682 for complete details.

Notes

Pros and Cons

Still can't figure out if this is the right school for you? You've already read through this in-depth guide; why not list the pros and cons? It will really help with narrowing down your decision and determining whether or not this school is right for you.

Pros	Cons

Notes

Need Help Paying For School?
Apply for our Scholarship!

College Prowler awards thousands of dollars a year to students who compose the best essays. E-mail *scholarship@collegeprowler.com* for more information, or call 1.800.290.2682.

Apply now at **www.collegeprowler.com**

Notes

Get Paid To Rep Your City!

Make money for college!

Earn cash by telling your friends about College Prowler!

Excellent Pay + Incentives + Bonuses

Compete with reps across the nation for cash bonuses

Gain marketing and communication skills

Build your resume and gain work experience for future career opportunities

Flexible work hours; make your own schedule

Opportunities for advancement

Contact *sales@collegeprowler.com*
Apply now at **www.collegeprowler.com**

Notes

Do You Own A Website?

Would you like to be an affiliate of one of the fastest-growing companies in the publishing industry? Our web affiliates generate a significant income based on customers whom they refer to our website. Start making some cash now! Contact *sales@collegeprowler.com* for more information or call 1.800.290.2682

Apply now at **www.collegeprowler.com**

Notes

Reach A Market Of Over 24 Million People.

Advertising with College Prowler will provide you with an environment in which your message will be read and respected. Place your message in a College Prowler guidebook, and let us start bringing long-lasting customers to you. We deliver high-quality ads in color or black-and-white throughout our guidebooks.

Contact Joey Rahimi
joey@collegeprowler.com
412.697.1391
1.800.290.2682

Check out **www.collegeprowler.com** for more info.

Notes

Write For Us!
Get Published! Voice Your Opinion.

Writing a College Prowler guidebook is both fun and rewarding; our open-ended format allows your own creativity free reign. Our writers have been featured in national newspapers and have seen their names in bookstores across the country. Now is your chance to break into the publishing industry with one of the country's fastest-growing publishers!

Apply now at **www.collegeprowler.com**

Contact *editor@collegeprowler.com* or call 1.800.290.2682 for more details.

Notes

Notes

Notes

Notes

Notes

Notes

Notes

Notes

Notes

Notes

Notes

Notes

Notes

Notes

Notes

Notes

Notes

Notes

Notes

Notes

Notes